Also available from Bloomsbury by Jeremy Black

Avoiding Armageddon
Contesting History
Crisis of Empire
Culture in Eighteenth-Century England
New Century War
Rethinking World War Two
The Great War and the Making of the Modern World
The Hanoverians
The War of 1812
Using History
War: A Short History
War and the New Disorder in the 21st Century

A Short History of Britain

Second Edition

JEREMY BLACK

Bloomsbury Academic
An imprint of Bloomsbury Publishing Plc

B L O O M S B U R Y
LONDON • NEW DELHI • NEW YORK • SYDNEY

Bloomsbury Academic

An imprint of Bloomsbury Publishing Plc

50 Bedford Square	1385 Broadway
London	New York
WC1B 3DP	NY 10018
UK	USA

www.bloomsbury.com

BLOOMSBURY and the Diana logo are trademarks of Bloomsbury Publishing Plc

First edition published by the Social Affairs Unit 2007

Second edition published by Bloomsbury 2015

© Jeremy Black, 2015

British Library Cataloguing-in-Publication Data
A catalogue record for this book is available from the British Library.

ISBN: HB: 978-1-4725-8665-0
PB: 978-1-4725-8666-7
ePDF: 978-1-4725-8667-4
ePub: 978-1-4725-8668-1

Library of Congress Cataloging-in-Publication Data
Black, Jeremy, 1955-
A short history of Britain / Jeremy Black.– Second edition.
pages cm
First edition published: 2007.
Includes bibliographical references and index.
1. Great Britain–History. I. Title.
DA30.B623 2015
941–dc23
2014030519

Typeset by Fakenham Prepress Solutions, Fakenham, Norfolk NR21 8NN
Printed and bound in India

For Jeannie Forbes

CONTENTS

PREFACE

A key player in world history, Britain has a history that touches, directly or indirectly, that of other countries around the world. Moreover, it is a history that repeatedly repays fresh examination, both because the present changes so frequently and because new perspectives emerge on the past. Writing in 2013–14, I face the possibility of the very dissolution of the British state, as Scotland may vote for independence in a referendum due in September 2014. Whether or not that happens, the very possibility of such an outcome reflects a markedly different present-day background to the past to that which would have been the case only 20 years ago. Indeed, the Scottish Parliament that helped make this referendum an issue was only established after a referendum following the Labour victory in the 1997 British general election, with the first elections for this Parliament held in 1999. In the event, independence was rejected by the voters.

I am very much aware of changing perspectives, not least because this process of change explains why it is necessary to have new histories, and also why individual historians need to reassess their own views and present their own work anew. There is a particular need for this in the case of national history; for, without any understanding of our past, we cannot appreciate our present or consider our future. History provides and explains identity, which is at once a key aspect of individuality and the cement of society; while collective memory is also a crucial focus of public education. This is because history is process as well as event: it is not simply a number of events in the past, but it is also an understanding today of how they were linked, and why, how and with what results, change occurred. In understanding the past, it is therefore possible to see history – change through time – as a process that encompasses us.

Moreover, reference to the past is a significant way of providing points of guidance as well as validation. Thus, the English barons drawing up demands on King John in 1215 used as their basis the coronation charter of Henry I (1100) which had promised to renounce the alleged abuses of his predecessor, William II, William Rufus (r. 1087–1100). In turn, Magna Carta, the name later given for the agreement John was obliged to accept in 1215, served in the early seventeenth century as the basis for constitutional opposition to claims and actions on behalf of the royal prerogative under James I (r. 1603–25) and Charles I (r. 1625–49). References continued. Charles, 11th Duke of Norfolk (1746–1815), a firm Whig, sought to commemorate the 600th anniversary of Magna Carta by building an octagonal Great Hall at his seat of Arundel Castle, a hall dedicated to 'Liberty asserted by the Barons in the reign of John'.

History therefore is about time; time as an enfolding context and change through time. This relationship is generally simplified in terms of structure and conjuncture or, phrased differently, circumstances and events. This is a dichotomy that does not do justice to the complexity of the dynamic of change, but one that has to stand, as a product of the extent to which we both express ourselves through language and are constrained by it.

In the case of Britain's history, the key structural elements are in part geographical and integral. The former are, most obviously, island status off the shore of a nearby continent, as well as the proximity of most of the country to the sea and to ports. There has also been, throughout human history in Britain, a generally benign climate, with plentiful rainfall and with only a limited period annually below freezing point. This situation has allowed agriculture without the organisational constraints of irrigation, as well as all-year-round fishing and shipping. There are, moreover, plentiful construction and power sources in terms of readily worked timber, stone, brick and coal.

The structural elements in British history are also a product of the development of a particular society and political culture. This development is complex and in part controversial, not least because discussion of it relates to issues of quality and approval, as well as the question of national exceptionalism or uniqueness. Nevertheless, the characteristic nature and role of law, property rights, family structure and political liberty are all crucial to British society and political culture. So also is a quest for freedom, however conditional it might in practice have been.

This point emerges clearly in the comparative context. Many of the ills, if not crimes, ascribed to Britain, particularly imperialism and the slave trade, were, in practice, far from unique to it; and much of the criticism is ahistorical, telling us far more about modern debates and issues than about the past. Indeed, to take these particular cases, the limited authority and power of government within Britain greatly affected the character of British imperialism, especially, but not only, in the case of colonies that received a large number of British settlers. Moreover, in the case of much of the empire, particularly India, areas that were conquered were frequently already ruled by other empires. Far, therefore, from Britain introducing some sort of poison of imperialism, it was frequently a case of one empire replacing another. Furthermore, while Britain, shamefully, was the leading participant in the terrible trans-Atlantic slave trade in the eighteenth century, Britain subsequently played the key role in ending the slave trade, the Royal Navy policing the Atlantic and Indian Oceans to that end during the nineteenth century.

In addition, Britain took the leading role against tyranny and aggression, both in opposition to Napoleon, a voraciously expansionist dictator of France (r. 1799–1815) who loved war, and to Germany in World Wars One and Two. The devotion of British and imperial energy and resources to defend freedom from Nazism in World War Two (1939–45) was a culmination, justification, and even a destiny for the British Empire. Whatever the slighting of the past and the inroads of revisionism, it is important to remember that individuals and society came together in these major challenges to save not only their country but also to make a key difference to the history of humanity. This collective belief, moreover, proved important to post-1945 British public culture, certainly until the 1960s when the certainties of the previous generation were challenged in a context of radical social and cultural change.

A focus on the particular character of British society and political culture permits and requires an overlap with conjunctures, not least in terms of how this political culture was obtained, secured and developed, why it became that of Britain, and what this meant for Britain and for the rest of the world. In the space of a short book, the challenge is how best to present these issues without the anachronism of Whiggish triumphalism, the sense that developments were inevitable, and that this is a cause of simplistic congratulation. However, the existence of that approach is itself part of the history of Britain. Indeed, Whiggish triumphalism was highly significant for the attitudes of many commentators in the eighteenth and nineteenth centuries.

Furthermore, it is necessary to address, in any history of Britain, the complexity of the relationship of this history with that of the British. These are understood in this history not as an ethnic or racial group, but as the inhabitants of Britain. This category included immigrants who came to Britain, as well as, far more indirectly, those who sailed forth and provided the bulk of the population of Australasia and Canada and much of that of the USA. The interactions between migration and both the structure and the conjunctures already referred to need to be addressed.

Invitations to speak at the Museum of London, at the Chalke Valley Literary Festival, and at Mary Washington University provided opportunities to develop some of the ideas offered here. I have benefited from the comments of John Blair, Bill Gibson, Bob Higham, Murray Pittock, Nigel Ramsay, Nigel Saul, Richard Toye and two anonymous readers on all or part of an earlier draft, and from the permission of Mike Mosbacher to use material already published by the Social Affairs Unit. It is a great pleasure to dedicate this book to Jeannie Forbes, a good and thoughtful friend.

CHAPTER ONE

Telling the story

History is bound up with questions of identity and value and, as these become more contentious, so the character of public history similarly is a matter of controversy. There was no period when this was not the case, but the issue has become more acute in recent years as national identity has appeared increasingly porous and, in some eyes, unclear. This situation has led to arguments in Britain (as elsewhere) for the affirmation of citizenship through public means. At one level, these means are controlling or proscriptive, as in proposals, in the 2000s and 2010s, for identity cards and for stronger immigration controls, and pressure for tests as conditions for citizenship.

At another level, these arguments relate to a probing of identity that is designed to elicit and understand common memories and assumptions. Historical awareness is very much bound up in this process. It is recognised as providing the context for these beliefs and assumptions, and also as channelling their expression, and thus affirming identity.

To write a short national history in this context is therefore a reckless undertaking if it is assumed that the project, or the response to it, can in some way be outside this background of contention. There are multiple sensitivities to consider. For Britain, some of the most obvious relate to its many pasts. For example, a poll conducted for the *BBC History Magazine*, and reported in its June 2006 issue, offered a choice of ten days for 'On what historical day do you think Britain should celebrate British Day?', and elicited the highest response for Magna Carta Day, 15 June. Magna Carta, the name subsequently given to the agreement forced from King John (r. 1199–1216) by baronial opponents in 1215, was a limitation in written form to royal rights. It thereby came to be seen as a charter of liberties. Magna Carta had a lasting resonance. Thus, on 12 March 2014, Tim Berners-Lee called on Radio Four for a 'Magna Carta-like Charter of Rights' to guarantee rights on the web. In practice, this charter of 1215, with its criticisms of the rule of John and its affirmation of a different standard of governance, was more directly English than a matter of Scottish or Welsh history. John ruled England, part of Wales, a smaller section of Ireland, and a decreasing number of French dominions; but he never ruled Scotland or all of Wales or Ireland.

Sensitivities are related to balance. How much space in this book should be devoted to Scottish or Welsh history, or indeed to the role of immigrants in British history over the last two centuries? What is the relevance of wider contexts, particularly that of Europe? Critiques of alleged bias and the very approach of balance, however, carry risks of their own. There is the problem of responding to apparent bias by producing a questionable new slant, as in neglecting to devote sufficient attention to England – which is a particular fault with the 'four nations' approach to British history, that of England, Scotland, Wales and Ireland.

There is also a general failure to devote sufficient attention to the localities and regions of England. Such attention needs to respond both to the changing role of regions but also to the varying significance of individual regions. For example, before the rise of coal-based industry in the late eighteenth century, the North of England, the West Midlands, the Central Belt of Scotland and South Wales were all less important (and in relative terms less populous) than they were to become. Instead, it was the South of England that was important, not only because it was the most fertile agricultural region but also because most political and governmental institutions were located there, as well as the naval bases, the English universities and the English centre of law and of publishing.

There is the separate problem that parcelling out geographical sections, however reasonably carried out, detracts attention from the overall English, or indeed, British, dimension of identity and experience. At the same time, the sense of changing local and regional settings for life both captured a key level of experience and contributed to discussion about how Britain was altering at the national level. Thus, W. Stanley Sykes, in his much reprinted *The Missing Money-Lender* (1931), referred to Barhaven, a fictional English manufacturing town where rapid, unplanned growth in the nineteenth century had left:

> dingy back-to-back houses crowded into courts and alleys of incredible ugliness with a complete disregard for light and air; noisy, smoky and odorous factories scattered at random among the residential parts of the town – all lay under a perpetual pall of smoke from the maze of chimney-pots.
>
> Desperate and expensive efforts were being made to rectify faults of fifty years' standing, and the twentieth-century pendulum had swung to the other extreme with a vengeance... Narrow streets which were death-traps to modern traffic were being widened at a fantastic cost.

And so on. The worked environment, like its built counterpart, reflected past and present, environmental pressures, economic opportunities and regulatory drives, all affecting the experience of those who worked and lived there.

As a separate issue, there is the more general question of the relationship between history as experience and history as causative process, and of how much attention should be devoted to each.

In Britain, the questions of national history and of causation were for long generally answered in terms of the Whig approach to history. This was an approach named after a British political party, and identified with a key political and intellectual tendency in the eighteenth and nineteenth centuries. The approach emphasised a Protestant identity for the nation, respect for property, the rule of law and parliamentary sovereignty as a means to secure liberty; and the approach combined a patriotic sense of national uniqueness with a frequently xenophobic contempt for foreigners. History was presented as moving in an inevitable direction and that being one of steady improvement; teleological progressivism in short.

In the dedication of 1760 for the fourteenth edition of his *A New History of England*, the prolific writer John Lockman, for example, 'endeavoured to set the whole in such a light as may inspire the readers with an ardent love for our pure religion, and its darling attendant, liberty; and, on the other hand, with a just abhorrence of popery [Catholicism], and its companion, slavery'. By slavery, British commentators referred to the situation in Britain and not across the empire, in short, political control, not the use of labour for economic purposes. Lockman's remarks captured the clear ideological framing of a sense of distinctive nationhood. This framing took place in large part in opposition to apparent threats, which reflected the extent to which responses to challenges were significant to national identity and to government policy.

The notions of progress inherent to this Whig approach could also be readily applied, both by contemporaries and, subsequently, to suggest modernisation in the eighteenth and early nineteenth centuries. In this account, superstition was banished and there was a 'big bang' of modernity, made up of the 'Glorious Revolution', religious toleration, the 'Age of Reason', the Industrial Revolution, the rise of the 'public sphere' – newspapers and coffee houses, and of democratic aspirations; and also a series of changes, including better communications (canals, turnpikes and postal services), that speeded up life and led to the spread of the news.

Challenging earlier historical views were an aspect of this approach. These challenges indicated the wider political context of historical opinions, both then and subsequently. For example, an editorial in the *Exeter Weekly Times* of 8 November 1828 began:

> The Gunpowder Plot.
> The return of the Fifth of November calls forth all over the country, for Protestant execration on Catholic bigotry; and the anniversary of a national deliverance is seized on, as a pretext for exciting by-gone prejudices for sowing dissentations, and inflaming ancient animosities. Catholic intolerance is descanted on by Protestant bigots, and ready invectives supply the place of historical truth. To how few, even among the liberals, have the real features of this conspiracy been lain open; and among the vulgar, who knows the gunpowder treason by any other name than the Popish Plot?

This reference to the 1605 conspiracy to blow up Parliament was particularly relevant in 1828 as debate was intense over Catholic Emancipation, the removal of legal disabilities on Catholics, a Whig policy that divided the rival Tories, then in government. The Catholic Emancipation Act was indeed passed in 1829.

Whiggism, certainly in the eyes of its supporters, was progressivism without autocracy or democracy, but this prospectus ceased to be a realistic option as democratic and populist politics became more important with the extension of the franchise (the right to vote). This was achieved for men, in part, with the Great or First Reform Act in 1832, but, more properly with its successors in the late nineteenth and early twentieth centuries, in 1867, 1884 and 1918. Furthermore, the two world wars destroyed much of the old social and political order, while the growth of popular purchasing power, and the resulting consumerist pressures, also served to foster change.

These changes had an impact on the content of the Whig approach of history. The narrative was changed and the earlier robustness of the approach was watered down, although important elements of this approach survived into the late twentieth century, and even to today. As another major shift, the teleological progressivism seen with the Whig approach was increasingly interpreted away from constitutional, political and imperial themes and, instead, toward notions of social progress and empowerment, which appeared to be more appropriate as themes for a democratic society committed to social welfare. This interpretation, however, left the constitutional and political dimension of public history unclear, which is an aspect of current disquiet over this dimension and over public history as a whole.

The validity of Whiggism as an interpretative tone, method and ideology is not the sole problem that has to be confronted when considering British history. In technical terms, the problem of content, of what a history book should discuss and the periodization that should be adopted, is linked to that of form, specifically the role of narrative and the relationship between cause and understanding. National histories tend to be narrative. Moreover, the combination of pressures for accessibility and having to cover a vast subject encourages a considerable degree of simplification.

This simplification, however, is problematic as it challenges the need to accept that there were, and are, various ways of understanding the past and explaining change. The relationship between structure and conjuncture referred to in the preface is one such. In this book, I do not seek to provide an easy narrative, but rather to remind readers of the unpredictabilities and indeterminacy that can be seen repeatedly in the history of the country and in attempts to explain it.

The present practice of disputing the national past – a practice that was in the spotlight in 2013 as revisions to the National Curriculum for history teaching in English and Welsh schools were debated – echoes earlier differences. In part, these very differences and debates are aspects of the national history, as are the marked changes in topic and tone that are involved. The topics to the fore in the consideration of national history have generally echoed the issues most urgent at the time.

Thus, the historicity, and therefore legitimacy, of the Protestant Church established in sixteenth-century England became a matter for debate between Protestant and Catholic controversialists. Seeking to minimise the role of the Papacy, Matthew Parker, Archbishop of Canterbury from 1559 to 1575, emphasised the antiquity of the British Church in his *De Antiquitate Britannicae Ecclesiae* (1572). Catholics, in contrast, stressed the conversion of Britain by St Augustine, who had been sent from Rome by Pope Gregory the Great in 597 and who converted the kingdom of Kent. Aethelbert, the king (r. *c.* 583–616), was rapidly converted, and he supported Augustine in establishing three bishoprics: at Canterbury, London and Rochester.

A poetic dimension to the historical presentation of the Reformation was offered by William Shakespeare (1564–1616) in his play *Henry VIII* (1613). During the first production of the play, the *Globe* theatre was burnt down as a result of the thatch catching light after cannon were fired to mark an entry of the actor playing the king. This deprived that audience of Archbishop Thomas Cranmer's (fictional) eulogy on the infant, born in 1533, who was to become Elizabeth I, a eulogy he was bid speak by Heaven, in which it was foretold that her virtues would be reborn, phoenix-like, in James I (r. 1603–25), then conveniently on the throne, and that:

> he shall flourish,
> And like a mountain cedar reach his branches
> To all the plains about him.

History, as thus staged, provided a glorious anticipation and justification of the present, a potent form of legitimation.

History, more generally, offered exemplary narratives that provided not only vindication but also an opportunity to place contemporary situations in historical contexts. Thus, for the Whigs of the early nineteenth century who pressed for parliamentary and other reform, it was possible to locate George III (r. 1760–1820) and George IV (r. 1820–30), both opponents of reform, as villains who were later versions of the dastardly Stuarts. The removal of James II (and VII of Scotland) in the Glorious Revolution of 1688–9 was regarded as the key founding episode of the Whig legacy.

The Whigs could also find heroes among their ancestors. In John, the sixth Duke of Bedford's Temple of Worthies at his stately home (country palace) at Woburn, a bust of Charles James Fox, the Whig leader, was present with those of Francis, the fifth Duke (1765–1802) and the sixth Duke (1766–1839), as well as such figures of Classical Roman probity as the Elder and Younger Brutus, all serving as remembrances of heroic virtue. A pediment by John Flaxman depicted Liberty and a frieze by Richard Westmacott the march of heroic virtue. Liberty was thus asserted and carefully grafted onto Whig family trees. Furthermore, the present was coined into historical myth, as with Fox, who, as soon as he died in 1806, gained iconic status, as seen in christening names as well as annual dinners.

Conversely, there was also serious criticism of the Whigs. To both radicals and Tories, they were the exponents of oligarchy. To Tories, moreover, Whigs, were the allies of radicalism, although, in fact, the Whigs had little time for radicalism.

Depiction of the past served not only different views on national politics but also the strategies of different interests, such as aristocratic families, town councils and individual families interested in their roots. These depictions could be contentious. For example, in the town of Taunton, 11 May, the anniversary of the raising of the siege of the Parliamentary-held stronghold in 1645 during the English Civil War, a result which was seen as a great providential salvation against the Royalists, was celebrated with sermons preached into the 1720s and an annual celebration into the 1770s. Politically, these events were a Nonconformist radical expression of opposition to the Tory Corporation (town government). These local politics relieved, and were enlivened by, historical divisions.

From the other end of the political spectrum, the celebration in the eighteenth century of the restoration of the Stuart dynasty in 1660 in the person of Charles II was a call for legitimism and for a second restoration, that of the exiled Stuart claimant to the throne and thus a criticism of the Hanoverian dynasty which ruled from 1714 to 1837.

Genealogy is currently the most popular form of history in Britain. When the National Archives put the 1901 census online, the pressure on the system was so intense that it crashed. Genealogy, however, is far from constant. An instructive sign of changing social mores is that most people by the 2000s did not seem to mind if they discovered that their ancestors were unmarried parents or illegitimate, and, in some cases, criminal. This attitude was very different from the traditional interest in lineage as a means to enhance family status through discovering distinguished and socially exalted forbears.

This point about family history is related to the more general issue of whose history is at stake. Whereas, until recently, the traditional pantheon of past rulers and military commanders dominated, more recently there has been a more varied emphasis. In 1999, the Royal Mail celebrated the Millennium with 48 stamps grouped in 12 'Tales': Inventors', Travellers', Patients', Settlers', Workers', Entertainers', Citizens', Scientists', Farmers', Soldiers', Christians' and Artists'. Five years later, the 150th anniversary of the start of British participation in the Crimean War with Russia (1854–6) was celebrated by printing stamps featuring not battles or generals, but ordinary soldiers, their images deriving from photographs taken in 1856 on their return from the war.

Similarly, recreations of the past in reality television, for example *1900 House* (1999), made the past comprehensible by involving a real family through the use of video-diary cameras. However, in practice, their responses told us more about their present-day views and dynamics. History cannot easily be relived.

Artistic presentations of national history also changed. Today, there is no comparison to the demand for empire seen with inter-war films such as *The Drum* (1938) and *The Four Feathers* (1939). Based on A.E.W. Mason's successful novel of 1902, the latter was a presentation (not the first) of recent imperial endeavour in Sudan (which Britain finally conquered in 1898–9) as a definition of manliness and heroism. Moreover, Richard Westmacott's 1839 relief carving, 'The Abolition of Suttee' (widow-burning) – for the pedestal of a statue of Lord William Bentinck, Governor-General of Bengal (1827–35) and first Governor-General of India (1833–5), like his 1829 portions of the monument in Calcutta Cathedral to Warren Hastings, who had earlier held similar posts, is an echo of an age-long past. Today, instead, there is a pervasive anti-imperial liberalism, which excludes earlier narratives of national glory through imperialism.

Far more radical voices receive little support in the world of film. For example, one of the few historical feature films ever to receive an endorsement from a senior historian was *Winstanley* (1975) by Kevin Brownlow and Andrew Mollo. This low-budget, independent film about Gerrard Winstanley, the leader of the radical mid-seventeenth century Digger movement, was recommended by the Marxist historian Christopher Hill, but it had only very limited release through film clubs. Conversely, criticisms of the British empire and of the nature of World War One, as in the successful musical and film, *Oh! What a Lovely War*, provided content and tone that would earlier have been generally unacceptable.

The Diggers have slight resonance in public memory. In contrast, both the Peasants' Revolt of 1381 and the Tolpuddle Martyrs of 1834 continue to be referred to, as in the 2000s, when the left-wing folk singer Roy Bailey and the left-wing politician Tony Benn toured with accounts of both.

Aside from issues of interpretation, knowledge of, and in, the past were, and are, far from constant. Printing and literacy were clearly important in shifts in the latter, but they were not alone. The visual understanding of the country also changed. 'Come, here is the map; shall we divide our right', said the Welsh leader Owen Glendower (Owain Glyndwr) to his fellow conspirators in William Shakespeare's play *Henry IV, Part 1* (1597). In practice, they would not have done so in 1403, when the conspiracy took place: maps were not then widely used, and were of insufficient quality to enable the detailed comments attributed to the conspirators. Nevertheless, to his late-sixteenth-century audience, benefiting from the advances of printing, which helped fix visual images, including maps, and also reflecting the greater use of maps in the Elizabethan period, it was perfectly credible that the three conspirators should refer to a map. Harry Hotspur is angry about the impact of the River Trent's course on his share:

Methink my moiety [share], north from Burton [on Trent] here,
In quantity equals not one of yours.

By 1900, thanks to mass education, knowledge of the country's
shape was much more widespread, providing a clear spatial context
for the understanding of the national past. This understanding,
however, has been eroded in recent decades as the appreciation of
physical geography and its effects has diminished. Motorways have
been punched through ranges of hills, with the M40, for example,
making the Chilterns appear no obstacle.

Shifts in popular interest and knowledge influence the context
within which historical perspectives could, and can, be grasped
and expressed. The frames of historical, geographical and cultural
reference have all changed greatly, and this affects both the understanding of the past and the exposition of it. At the same time, part
of the fascination of the past is what it tells us about a changing
present.

CHAPTER TWO

The history to 1400

One useful approach to the history of Britain is to argue that its fundamentals had been settled by 1400. If a long-term geopolitical, political and constitutional viewpoint is adopted, these fundamentals would be seen to lie in an independent English state (that included Wales), separate from an independent Scottish state. In both, there were limits to royal power and authority. In England, there was a well-developed representative system in the shape of Parliament, while freedoms were grounded in the Common Law. Such an approach, with its emphasis on origins and early developments, corresponds to the focus on early republican history, specifically the Founding Fathers, in American history. This focus in American history, however, has been recently challenged by a different narrative that concentrates on later immigration, civil rights, and the history of the last century-and-a-half.

Although the time-scale and content and context are different, a similar challenge to the conventional long-term account of national history has occurred in Britain. This challenge focuses on a later period. It begins with the creation of national identity and institutions from the late seventeenth century, notably the Glorious Revolution of 1688–9, and the parliamentary union of England (including Wales) and Scotland in 1707. Imperial expansion, industrial transformation, and subsequent social and political change, all emerge as crucial in this account. An even later challenge centres on the age of mass democracy that began in the late nineteenth century, and on the accompanying social developments.

While capturing the significance of these periods, an account focusing on post-1688 or on post-1884 underrates the importance of earlier centuries. Moreover, as history, it is not an account that would have made much sense in Scotland or England in the nineteenth century, or indeed earlier. In fact, there was in the nineteenth century a strong feeling that earlier history was part of the cause and, thus, the battleground of British liberties, and was accordingly highly relevant to them. 'British' was largely understood as English, but with a separate Scottish narrative.

Alfred, King of Wessex (r. 871–99), shared with the more obscure, possibly early sixth-century, warlord King Arthur the happy role for England of providing distinguished ancestry for notions of valiant liberty; although, with the idea of the 'Norman yoke', it was believed that these had been pushed aside in England by the Norman Conquest of 1066, and had had to be recovered. Magna Carta (1215) played a key role in the account of this recovery.

Paintings such as Daniel Maclise's *Alfred the Great in the Camp of the Danes* (1852) reflected the demand for an exemplary national history on canvas. This demand was seen also in his grand frescoes, *Wellington and Blücher at Waterloo* (1861) and *The Death of Nelson* (1864), painted for the new Palace of Westminster that was built after Parliament burned down as the result of an accident in 1834. In 1873, the carving of a white horse in a hillside near Westbury that was believed to commemorate Alfred's victory over the Danes at Ethandune in 878 was restored. It could – and can still – be seen, recently restored anew, by the passengers on the Great Western Railway between London and the West Country. In Scotland, William Wallace (d. 1305) and Robert the Bruce (1274–1329), medieval leaders of the independence struggle against England, were similarly celebrated as heroes, being presented as having made possible the 1707 union of England and Scotland from a position of two independent states.

Such celebrations were longstanding. In the mid-fifteenth century Henry VI of England (r. 1422–61, 1470–1) had backed the canonisation of Alfred, in order to provide validation for a view of the longevity of English kingship. Moreover, in the eighteenth century, notably the late 1730s, Alfred was presented as a worthy exemplar of national kingship by critics of George II, a member of the Hanoverian dynasty that had come from Germany in 1714.

Whether the subsequent interpretative emphasis is on the politics and warfare in, and with, which independence and liberties were contested from the fifth to the seventeenth centuries, or on the socio-economic changes of the last three centuries, it is also necessary, in charting the history of Britain, to consider the long-term struggle to adapt to the possibilities and problems of the environment. In this struggle, Britain shared in wider developments and that is the appropriate start.

Prior to the Romans

The first evidence of early man in Britain comes from about 90,000 years ago from a site in Norfolk where footprints (lost within a few weeks) were found on a beach in 2013. Rather than continuous settlement, a number of periods of settlement are now assumed: periods linked to the retreats of the polar ice. When the climate permitted, early man spread from southern to northern Europe, probing the arctic tundra. Human remains of early hominids and finds of tool assemblages have been found in many sites in southern England, for example in Stoke Newington, part of modern London. It was announced in May 2014 that in Vauxhall, also in modern London, Stone Age finds included a fish trap, man-made pits, a chopping tool, a scraping tool, burnt animal bone fragments, and signs of burnt ground, indicating campfires. It is thought that early human species camped on the foreshore and on gravelly river islands on the River Thames.

The Neanderthals were replaced by anatomically modern humans during the Upper Palaeolithic period (*c.* 35,000 to *c.* 12,000 years ago); and this period saw a development of social structures and stone blade technology. Following the end of the last Ice Age in about 10,000 BC, a northward movement of forest and wildlife led to the spread of deciduous trees, such as oak, elm, ash and lime, to an increase in animal and plant life, and to more opportunities for hunter-gatherers.

As the ice melted, the sea level rose, anticipating what might be the consequences of present-day global warming. In about 6500 BC, the land-bridge that joined England to the Continent across the southern North Sea was cut, a key development in British history, and certainly the fundamental event in its historical geography. As an island, or rather an archipelago (group of islands), Britain was harder to invade, while maritime trade was to be a key feature in national development.

Domestic crops arrived in Britain in the fifth millennium BC, in about 4200 BC, providing a more settled human imprint centred on farming, which permitted a larger production of food than hunter-gathering. In turn, this production and settlement encouraged a more developed material culture and more trade. The spread of domestic animals (cattle, sheep, pigs, horses and oxen) was followed by wheeled vehicles. As the population rose, evidence of settlements increased, while trackways developed, for example the 'Sweet Track' across the Somerset Levels constructed in about 3800 BC. The shift to farming led to the widespread clearing of woodland in the second millennium BC, although woodland remained a major resource. Wood was the source of fuel and building material. A set of small gold bracelets found near Lydney in the Forest of Dean in 2013 have been assessed as likely to have belonged to the children of a local chieftain. They reflect the extent of social ranking that had already emerged between 1500 and 1100 BC.

The most famous legacy of the period is Stonehenge, a ritual centre that developed in phases. It took possibly two million man-hours to complete (by *c.* 1550 BC), and the blue stones came from as far as Wales. The effort and organisation necessary for such a work was formidable. The nature of the religious beliefs linked to Stonehenge is unclear, but they were clearly related to astronomical observations. Recent archaeological work suggests that there were two centres there, one for the dead and one for the living, with evidence of plentiful feasting at the latter. It is indicative of the changing experience of the past that Stonehenge is now largely seen through car windows by people stuck in slow traffic on the A303.

Metalworking spread into southern England by the third millennium BC, part of the process of Britain sharing in European developments. The Copper Age was followed from 2300 BC by that of Bronze, and from 700 BC by that of Iron. Iron tools, such as hoes and nails, brought new possibilities to agriculture and construction, and also encouraged trade.

Iron Age society in England was different from that of its nemesis, imperial Rome. There were proto-towns, known to the Romans as *oppida*, but not a developed urban civilization; and states, but not a sophisticated governmental system. There was no written culture, and, instead of there being one language, language was divisive. Yet there had also been considerable development. Much of the woodland, particularly in southern England, had been cleared of trees, and agriculture supported a growing population, a settled society and an aristocratic élite. Moreover, there was a coinage.

There was, however, in what was very much a tribal society, no sign of any identity that might be termed Britain, England, Scotland or Wales, nor any state or federation of states coterminous with any of them, nor any uniformity of conditions within what would later be these areas; although the evidence does not permit the denial of these possibilities. The concept of firm territorial boundaries in this period is not a helpful one. The number of surviving forts, walls and ditches suggests that conflict was frequent and life precarious. Massacre sites such as Fin Cop, from about 400 BC, and Danebury, from about 100 BC, provide further indication of this frequency.

It is unclear what would have happened to England but for the Roman conquest. Ireland and the areas of Germany and Scotland that were not conquered by Rome were essentially to develop into a number of small kingdoms that focused on farming but also took part in trade. Prior to the Roman conquest, southern Britain was already linked by trade to nearby areas of the Continent. Indeed, in some respects, bar for Christianity, the post-Roman Britain of the seventh century AD was similar to that of the late Iron Age.

Roman Britain

The situation across much of Britain, however, was to be transformed as a result of Roman conquest which, in AD 43–83, led to the overrunning of England, Wales and southern Scotland. Earlier, after Julius Caesar had rapidly conquered Gaul (France), he had turned his attention to Britain, in part because he argued, with some reason, that support from Britain was responsible for continuing resistance in Gaul, and in part for personal reasons: to acquire glory and to keep the army under his control active. In his expeditions in 55 and 54 BC, he took advantage of power-struggles within Britain, but faced unexpectedly strong resistance as well as storms. In 54 BC, Caesar crossed the river Thames and seized the capital, possibly in the area of Wheathampstead, of the regional tribal leader, Cassivellaunus.

Nevertheless, Caesar's expedition had no immediate consequences, in part because the Roman empire had first been convulsed by civil wars and then by expansion on the more threatening Rhine frontier. Instead, trade links developed with Britain, as did political relationships.

It was the Emperor Claudius, a far less impressive figure than Caesar, who, in AD 43 launched Rome into the conquest of Britain, both to gain a military reputation judged necessary to strengthen his position and because Rome's protégés in southern Britain had lost control. South-east England was overrun that year, the South and the Midlands rapidly following. However, a major uprising in AD 60 under Boudicca, the mistreated Queen of the Iceni tribe in modern East Anglia, proved a serious challenge. The major Roman settlements in Britain, which were then Colchester, St Albans and London, were destroyed and their inhabitants were slaughtered. Boudicca was then defeated by Gaius Suetonius Paulinus, the Roman Governor, at an unknown site, possibly in the Midlands.

The Romans pressed on to conquer northern England and to invade Scotland, although they were only able to conquer southern Scotland and that briefly. Instead, the northern frontier of Roman Britain depended for much of its history on Hadrian's Wall, a stone wall, supported by fortresses, stretching all the way from the Solway Firth to the North Sea close to Newcastle. What might have been a lasting division of Britain at this line, however, was not to be, because Roman rule was eventually to cease in England.

Outside the towns, which were the centres of authority, consumption and Roman culture, including, eventually, Christianity, Roman Britain was not as thoroughly Romanised as other provinces such as France and Spain. A level of foreign settlement and culture was superimposed on a society much of which remained true to its agrarian roots and which largely lacked the townships that *Romanitas* particularly required. As a result, the long-term political and cultural consequences of Roman rule were less than they might have been.

Britain under the Roman empire, however, shared a wider prosperity that, in part, reflected greater opportunities for trade. Mining and agriculture developed, and the greater quantity of archaeological material surviving from the Roman period suggests a society producing and trading far more goods than its Iron Age predecessor. Transport improvements and the need to supply cities – notably Londinium (London), which was probably settled from about AD 50 – brought out the possibilities for economic specialisation offered by the development of networks of exchange in Britain. These networks were seen in particular in the Greater London area, with the role of the rural hinterland as supplier of food and other resources to London, supplies organised by the smaller towns of the region such as Staines, Brentford and Ewell. London was the centre for the province's overseas trade. Leading exports from Britain included grain, woollen goods and hunting dogs; while imports included consumer goods, notably wine, glass, pottery, marble, olive oil and the preserved fish sauce called garum that was important to the Roman diet.

From London, roads built by the Romans radiated across Roman Britain. Reflecting the quality of Roman engineering and planning, and the lack of any need to consider land ownership, these roads were built straight and to a high standard, with stone foundations and gravel surfaces. Among these roads, Watling Street went to Chester, Ermine Street to York, and Stane Street to Chichester. London was also a river port, like the Roman cities of York, Lincoln, Chester and Gloucester. Such cities reflected the urban basis of authority under the Romans.

The arrival and spread of Christianity continued the pattern of cultural and institutional links with the Continent that was already seen with earlier religions under the Romans, notably the Olympian cults and that of Mithras. Shrines, temples and churches were very much located in the cities. Indeed, the urban nature of religious activity was an important characteristic of the Roman period.

Britain was affected by the growing crisis of the Roman empire in the fourth century as it came under pressure from 'barbarian invaders, notably in 342–3, 360 and 367–8. In southern Britain, these attacks came from the Saxons of north-west Germany. The attacks led, in the third century, to the construction of a series of coastal forts on what was known as the Saxon Shore. Moreover, the walls of cities such as London were strengthened.

The archaeological record suggests decline. For example, for London in the later fourth century, coinage finds are lower than would have been anticipated on the basis of earlier finds. Moreover, the distribution of late Roman finds in London suggests that much of the western half of the city was more or less abandoned.

400–800

Roman rule came to an end in AD 406–10. There was no dramatic 'barbarian' attack, but, rather, an end of political links with Rome as a result of internal dissension within the empire. The Romano-Britons overthrew the administration of Constantine III, a usurper, and appealed to the true emperor, Honorius, for the restoration of legitimate rule, but, under pressure from invasion by the Huns, he could do no more than tell them to look to their own defence. St Germanus, Bishop of Auxerre, who visited Britain in 429 to combat the Pelagian heresy, which denied the doctrine of original sin, noted that cities were surviving, but that their defence was in local hands rather than those of Roman troops. From mid-century, however, the situation appears to have deteriorated as a result of 'barbarian' invasion. Indeed, in about 446, an unsuccessful appeal for help was sent to Rome, which, however, again was in no position to send assistance.

The collapse of the Roman order was followed by Britain returning to a subsistence economy and a probably violent society, with few ceramics or coins in the archaeological record. The latter, however, poses problems, being greatly affected by the nature of the material culture and, in particular, the reliance on wood. This is not the sign of a primitive society, but it ensures that there are few remains of buildings from the period. The problems of excavating ephemeral timber structures were particularly serious before new techniques were developed in the 1930s. In addition, the remains in cities were affected by later building work, and by the destruction of material in centuries of cellaring.

Nevertheless, cross-sections of the archaeological record in cities such as Exeter and London provide clear evidence of discontinuity in settlement. Part of this was presumably the result of conflict between Britons, rather than the assault on them by invaders. A major cause of the fifth-century instability was probably that British inhabitants of the more upland areas, which were less

Romanised in the civil sense, retained much more idea of fighting and using weapons in their own traditional ways, and therefore found the Romanised lowlanders very easy victims once imperial power was withdrawn.

These lowlanders may have been identified as peoples, and organised as polities, on the basis of late Roman city-territories and dioceses; or the process of identification and organisation may have involved less continuation. The extent to which British society was influenced by Rome is unclear.

Invasion of Britain by those who had never been Romanised at all was, in the event, a far more serious and successful challenge. Angle and Saxon invaders from Denmark and Germany came to dominate England: the Angles in the North (Northumbria), the Midlands (Mercia) and East Anglia; the Saxons in the South. The Jutes settled in Kent. Christianity withered in the face of the pagan invaders, although their occupation of an already managed landscape helped ensure a significant degree of continuity. Although, in about 500, the resistance achieved a major victory, possibly under a warrior called Artorius (Arthur) at Mons Badonicus, the Britons were gradually driven back into Wales, Cumbria and Cornwall. The Britons fled, or survived as slaves and peasants acculturated to a militarily dominant invading élite.

The areas of settlement initially reverted to those of the pre-Roman centuries. Links with the Continent were greatly frayed, and trade was far less significant than it had been for the economy of Roman Britain. Anglo-Saxon settlers not only concentrated on agriculture, but also were largely self-sufficient. Anglo-Saxon rulers initially did not live within the Roman city walls.

The Scots, who were originally from Ireland, as the DNA evidence shows, may have been for a long time on both sides of the North Channel. They became increasingly important in Scotland, absorbing, by the late eighth century, the Picts, who had successfully resisted the Romans and who occupied the lands north of the Firth of Forth.

The invaders of Britain, Roman and non-Roman, however, were not successful without struggle, nor, indeed, everywhere. Cornwall was only conquered by the Saxons in 838, and the kingdoms in Wales were not conquered at all, although pressure from Mercia shaped the extent of Wales.

In time, there was a resumption of much that was associated with Roman and sub- or post-Roman Britain. Indeed, modern advances in archaeology, notably the large-scale funding of research archaeology from the 1970s, have filled in some of the gaps in the record and suggest that there was more activity than hitherto believed, for example in London.

Moreover, conversion to Christianity, by missionaries originally from Rome or Ireland, mostly in the seventh century, was important in aligning Britain culturally far more closely with the Continent. This missionary activity drew on the energy and wealth of the Kentish and Northumbrian royal dynasties respectively. The cultural alignment with the Continent was particularly based on the Kentish and East Anglian kingdoms.

Christianity also meant a spread of education and literacy, and the beginnings of written law, which served to convey rights in land. Society was becoming partly institutionalised, certainly in comparison with the fifth and sixth centuries. Town life also resumed or became more active. Place-name and other evidence indicate a spread of settlement and cultivation. Alongside towns there were *wics* or market exchange centres.

Christianisation was an aspect of major change in the period from *c.* 590, which therefore acts as a watershed. The other major indicators are a series of very rich princely graves, most prominently Sutton Hoo, as well as princely grand halls, notably Yeavering. The characteristics of the latter two developments were wealth and stratification. The change in the archaeological record suggests a sudden and spectacular concentration of wealth and raw materials in fewer hands. This may be linked to economic changes, notably an increase in exports to the Continent, and, accordingly, in trading settlements. Woollen cloth, lead and slaves were exported. This was related to the availability of Byzantine gold in Francia in the late sixth century, gold that was used to buy English products. As a result, gold came into England and is found in the grave goods at Sutton Hoo.

Spectacular funerals and grand halls were aspects of display in a society that was at once wealthy and competitive. Most graves after *c.* 600 did not have grave goods, but those of the princes were different. Interest in Roman civilisation was another aspect of this competitive display by and among rulers, and this interest meant Christian civilisation. The positive response by Anglo-Saxon rulers to missionary activity reflected this situation and contrasted with the fifth and sixth centuries, when a chaotic and highly fragmented society had not been attractive for missionary activity from Rome.

Particular wealth came from the scale and importance of English wool exports. Extensive metal-detector finds in the 1990s and 2000s have revealed that the volume of coinage in the early eighth century was very high in eastern and southern England. There were about 30 million coins in circulation in England in *c*. 720, and these coins were distributed very widely across the countryside. Far from being an élite or controlled currency, coins were used by many to participate both in local trade and in the very extensive trade across the Channel and the North Sea.

London, Ipswich, Sandwich in Kent and Southampton developed as ports in the seventh and eighth centuries. Excavations in Covent Garden in the 2000s produced finds from the early Saxon period of the late sixth or seventh century, but mostly from post-650 with a heyday in the early eighth. Writing in the 730s, Bede, a Northumbrian monk, described London as 'a mart of many peoples', while already, in the 670s, London had been referred to in a charter as a place 'where ships land'. This expansion was linked to a change in bullion supplies and trade links. Due to changes in Continental power politics and trade routes, the availability of gold dried up by the late seventh century. In its place, there was a silver economy, with the silver coming from the Harz mountains in Germany. Trade with the Low Countries and the Rhineland rose accordingly, and, on the English side, the ports referred to developed in an age of emporia.

The southern North Sea served as a unifier by the late seventh century. This was linked to a division within England. The eastern part was closely linked to this North Sea economy, while the western part, though politically English, in that it was ruled by Anglo-Saxon monarchs, was still in many ways British, in that its society still showed much continuity with post-Roman Britain.

In the eighth century, the major development in trade was linked to that in settlements and in agrarian practices. The latter included the spread of significant innovations, notably more intensive weeding and manuring and the use of corn-dryers and water-mills.

Communication problems helped shape the country very differently from today. Valleys were prone to flood, and their clay soil was often heavy, poorly drained and difficult to traverse. Instead, most land routes sought to follow ridges where the soil was drier. Bridging points, such as London, and ferries took central roles in the communication system. The greater role of bridges is suggested by the extent to which, from the 740s, labour service for bridge-building and repair became an important provision in charters. The difficulties of land transport, not least the draft animals required to pull laden wagons, led to an emphasis on water transport; and places where major land and water routes intersected were of great potential significance. In the Anglo-Saxon period, a key movement of wool was from the Cotswolds towards the south-east via the Thames water-system.

In England, Wales and Scotland, there was a coalescence of the numerous small kingdoms, initially probably based on successful warbands, into larger kingdoms, and this coalescence was also linked to institutional development and to the emergence of settlements with a higher status. Particularly after *c.* 700, ruling houses, such as the West Saxon kingdom of Wessex, based in Hampshire and the West Country, were increasingly differentiated from landowners, and royal justice was to be distinguished from that of kin, feud and surety. Justice was also differentiated from might.

Initially, Kent and East Anglia were the most important distinct kingdoms. The influence of Kent ensured that Canterbury, its capital, became the key early site of Christian conversion. As a result, Canterbury, not London, was the see of the Archbishop. However, the search for hierarchy and dominance among the Anglo-Saxon polities encouraged warfare and political change in which the respective position of the kingdoms changed. Kent declined.

The Kings of Northumbria, who ruled between the Humber and the Forth in eastern Britain and between the Mersey and the Ayr on the west, were dominant for most of the seventh century and were at times treated as overlords by the other English rulers, and by those of Scotland. In 685, however, the Picts defeated and killed King Ecgfrith of Northumbria at Nechtansmere (which may have been in Strathspey), a crucial event in the establishment of the relationship between what were to become England and Scotland.

Northumbrian hegemony was replaced by that of the Midlands kingdom of Mercia, especially under King Offa (757–96). During his reign, the frontier with Wales was defined with the consolidation of Offa's Dyke (r. *c.* 784–96). This earthwork network both consolidated existing earthworks and added new ones. Radiocarbon dating has revealed sections of the earthworks dating from 430 to 652, in other words from before Offa's reign. The term 'Wales' emerged from the Old English term for Romans, *wealas*, and was increasingly applied as if it was a description of the British lands west of Mercia, these lands being the largest bloc of British kingdoms.

Offa extended his power over south-east England, and the speech/dialect of the London area, like those of Oxford and the South Midlands, derives from Mercian forms of English. The role of London probably affected the dynamics of Mercia. Its heartland in the north-west Midlands was not monetarised, but access to London provided control over a wealthy area with much money. Offa's authority was maintained by his successor, Cenwulf (r. 796–821), who harshly suppressed a rebellion in Kent in 798, issued several charters from London, and suspended Archbishop Wulfred of Canterbury. However, Mercia was then challenged by the rise of the kingdom of Wessex. In 825, following victory at Ellandun over the Mercians, Egbert, King of Wessex conquered south-east England.

At the same time, the Church encouraged a sense of English identity. The canons of the Synod of Hertford (672) were issued for, and applied to, the entire English Church, and Bede, a Northumbrian monk, wrote his *Ecclesiastical History of the English People* in 731. He presented the English as one Christian people. Subsequent ecclesiastical writers continued with this theme, and it was to be strengthened by the experience of pagan attack by the Vikings, attack which was particularly felt in the monasteries, the centres of Anglo-Saxon culture.

Englishness was also used as a form of identity that transformed what was by modern standards a multicultural society of Britons, Romans, Angles, Saxons and Jutes into a unity in which ethnic origin was far less important than the shared experience of living in England. Within Anglo-Saxon England, the Britons ceased to have any distinctive separate identity: they formed the peasantry, with the exception of those who intermarried with the Anglo-Saxons. Although all such comparisons risk being ahistorical, there is the possibility of an interesting parallel between the ethnic integration of the first millennium with the situation today, although with the significant proviso that, once Christianisation had become the norm, religious issues apparently did not challenge integration as they do today.

800–1066

By the end of Offa's reign, the Vikings, raiders from Scandinavia, had arrived. Although initially only raiders, they soon posed a challenge that was much more abrupt than that mounted by the Anglo-Saxons in the fifth century. The Vikings were a presence across Britain, the Norse (Norwegians) particularly important on the north and west coasts of Scotland, while the Danes overran much of England, conquering East Anglia (865), Yorkshire (866–7), and Mercia (877), before being defeated by Alfred of Wessex in 878 at Ethandune (Edington) in Wiltshire. This success was underwritten in 879 when the Danish Great Army left to seek opportunities on the Continent. Alfred then campaigned into south-east England, occupying London.

Alfred's reign and those of his able successors, particularly Edward the Elder (r. 899–924) and Athelstan (r. 924–39), were important in the development of an English identity. They defeated and drove back the Danes, conquering the Midlands and, with greater difficulty, the north of England. As a result, Eadred (r. 946–55) could be described as the first king of the English, while, in 973, Edgar (r. 959–75) was the first to be crowned as king of the English. The earlier destruction of the other Anglo-Saxon ruling houses by the Danes allowed Alfred and his successors to be portrayed as English rather than merely West Saxon kings – although, in one light, Mercia and the North were conquered by the House of Wessex.

Alfred, who was an active patron of a Court culture that extolled his value, presented himself as the champion of Christianity and of all Anglo-Saxons against the pagan Danes. He was the crucial figure in the shift towards a new politics and a new kingdom, the Old English kingdom. This was a state that did not require precise ethnic or geographic borders. The eroding of the distinction between Mercia and Wessex was particularly notable in the development of this kingdom. Further from the centre of power in Wessex, Northumbria retained a greater sense of difference.

The expanding state also developed internally, a process pushed hard by Alfred and his successors. Most significantly, there was the consolidation of a county or shire system, public courts as a link between rulers and free men, and an effective means of assessment for taxation and military service. *Burhs*, fortresses or enclosures, were founded by Alfred and his successors not only as military bases but also as towns that both anchored royal authority and forwarded economic activity. The location and growth of *burhs* were also related to developments in the transport system, with, for example, the establishment of a *burh* at Oxford linked to the construction of a bridge across the River Thames. The overall significance of urban activity increased. By 1066, about 10 per cent of the English population lived in towns, which were more clearly under royal government than rural areas.

The improvement of the coinage, with Alfred responsible for a new standard for the penny, indicated that this was not rule by warrior band and that the government had considerable sophistication. At the same time, there is considerable controversy over the nature, power and stability of the Old English state. An emphasis on Old English strength suggests that the origins of modern England can be located in this state, a view that encourages a stress on the longevity of England and its institutional origins in the participatory system of Old English public courts. Conversely, it is also possible to question both points, not least by querying the power of the Old English state in northern England and the extent to which it did more than overawe contrary tendencies.

The idea of Old English statehood can in part be reconceptualised as that of a far-flung kingship that covered essentially the area of modern England, but it is unclear how far this led to a concept of Englishness and the English nation as matching these bounds. The political language of the Old English state served to include peoples of differing ethnic background who, moreover, had been under different rulers. The language of national sentiment can be seen in the poem that commemorated the battle of Maldon with the Danes in 991 (an honourable defeat), as well as with the treatment of some saints as national figures; but the extent to which these views were widely held is unclear. At the same time, the idea of any national identity without qualification, indeed contradiction, is somewhat farfetched. By the standards of the age, the Old English monarchy ruled what was an effective and powerful state. As a result, the political, constitutional and governmental history of England can be readily traced to the ninth century. Effective royal justice combined with a system of law-courts was important to the development of English law, both then and in the long term.

A related debate focuses on the nature of military power, not least its dependence on public authority, and the extent to which there was a nation in arms as opposed to a high-status warrior army. All freemen were in theory obliged to serve in the *fyrd* or army, which certainly suggests such authority. However, the roles of lords, their retinues and landholding were all important, and the core of armies raised on a shire base probably came from the landholding class. There was also a tradition, from the 990s onwards, of using taxation to pay for trained mercenaries in royal service.

The same processes could be seen with Kenneth MacAlpin (d. 858), who became ruler of the Scots and Picts in about 843, and with his descendants. As in England, the Church brought ideological and administrative support to the monarchy in Scotland, and government became more systematic. However, Scotland was poorer than England and its government less developed. Moreover, much of modern Scotland, including the area centred on the Moray Firth, let alone lands further north and west, resisted control. The dynasty was more interested in expanding south, overrunning Strathclyde early in the tenth century and Lothian later that century. This process was helped by the degree to which there was no obvious geographical boundary between Scotland and England, and no ethnic unity to either. What eventually became Scotland included Scots, Picts, Angles and Britons, and, until the mid-twelfth century, it was unclear whether Cumbria and Northumbria would be part of England or of Scotland. That the kings of Scotland were to owe fealty and homage to the kings of England for lands they held in northern England subsequently complicated the situation. Scotland did not abandon the northern countries until the Quitclaim, or Treaty, of York in 1237.

Under its unimpressive ruler, Aethelred the Unready, the English state was challenged by the Danes in the 990s and 1000s, and finally overthrown by large-scale Danish attack in the 1010s. The weaknesses of the state included a divided nobility, while Aethelred was no Alfred; but the Danish assault was particularly strong. Like England, Denmark had benefited from a measure of political and governmental development. In 1016, Cnut, the younger son of King Sweyn Forkbeard of Denmark, became ruler of England: earlier in the year, he had partitioned it with Aethelred's son, Edmund Ironside. Edmund received Wessex, and Cnut Mercia, but Edmund had then died.

Ruled astutely by Cnut until his death in 1035, England became, from 1019, part of a multiple kingdom that included Denmark and, later, Norway. This was an Anglo-Danish rule. Unlike earlier invaders, Cnut seized a kingdom of England. Cnut established his own supporters on the land, but there was no mass expropriation of Anglo-Saxon landlords, and Cnut was careful to maintain close links with the powerful monasteries.

Cnut's warring successors, his sons, the half-brothers Harold Harefoot and Harthacnut, were unable to maintain family unity, let alone the Anglo-Danish state, which was permanently divided. In England, the house of Wessex was restored with ease in 1042. The new monarch, King Edward 'the Confessor', who revived the Old English monarchy, was chosen king by popular acclamation in London. The expression of the view of the citizens in London in the royal succession, already seen after the deaths of Cnut and Harold Harefoot, demonstrated that a citizen body existed.

In 1051–2, in turn, Edward faced a challenge from the most powerful noble, Earl Godwin of Wessex. Edward lacked children, the essential attribute of dynastic success. This ensured a contested succession after he died in 1066. Edward's relative, Duke William of Normandy, competed with Edward's brother-in-law, Godwin's eldest son, Earl Harold of Wessex, while Harald Hardrada, King of Norway, also advanced a claim. In what was to be a year of three kings (like 1483 and 1936), Harold became King with the support of the bulk of the English aristocracy and having been designated by Edward.

However, William and Harald both prepared to invade. In response to William's preparations, Harold deployed his forces on the south coast, but Harald, not William, invaded first, landing close to York and defeating the local forces on 20 September at Fulford Gate. Harold then rapidly marched north, surprising, defeating and killing Harald at the battle of Stamford Bridge outside York on 24 September. Four days later, however, William landed on the south coast. Harold rapidly marched south and the two clashed at Hastings on 14 October.

This was a hard-fought battle between two effective systems, and its outcome was far from certain, although the Normans had key advantages in archers and cavalry. Eventually, the outnumbered English defensive shieldwall, well-deployed on a ridge, was disrupted by attacks designed to exploit real or feigned retreats by the Normans, and, at last, the English position was broken.

Harold's death was crucial, both in helping what became the final Norman assault in the battle and in ensuring its aftermath. Helped by a collapse of the resolve of the defeated English élite, William rapidly exploited his victory to advance on London and seize the throne, becoming William I, and going down in history as William the Conqueror. A high level of tension was indicated when the acclamation of William as king by the English in the abbey church at Westminster led Norman troops outside to fear opposition, and they reacted by setting fire to several buildings and killing some of the bystanders.

1066–1200

Norman rule was followed by the Normanisation of England, with powerful political, social, ecclesiastical and cultural pulses from the Continent active in the shadow of the new regime. English opposition was suppressed, brutally so in the North, which, in response to a rebellion, was 'harried' in 1069–70. The last major rebellion was in 1075. Moreover, the new order was entrenched by numerous castles, such as the White Tower of what became the Tower of London, and the new castle on the Tyne at what became the city of Newcastle. Early Norman castles were generally motte-and-bailey, earth and timber constructions, thrown up in a hurry (although still requiring many man-days to construct) and able to give protection against local discontent; though some were built of stone. Castle design was intended to promote a powerful symbol of the new authority over native society, as well as of the powers of the new landholding families in relation to each other. William I (r. 1066–87) and his successors also maintained castles in the shire towns, such as Exeter and Nottingham (as well as in London), as part of their framework of royal government.

The new landed order was one in which land was awarded to vassals in return for military service. Norman lords were obliged to provide a number of knights (as likely to fight on foot as on horseback) for military service roughly proportionate to the size of the lord's estate. This obligation was usually discharged by enfeoffing the required number with lands of their own in return for service. To historians, this was a system described as feudalism, although contemporaries did not perceive it in such systemic terms. Although feudalism is sometimes contrasted starkly with what went before, there was, in fact, an overlap with Anglo-Saxon practices. Moreover, the conferring of land and status was a response to public office as well as military assistance.

An instance of royal authority and power was provided by the compiling of the remarkably detailed *Domesday Book* (1086–8), the first attempt by an English monarch to establish the ownership and value of landed property across the country. It drew on the testimony of local people, but also on the documentation of landownership produced for local sheriffs prior to the Norman Conquest. Thus, *Domesday Book* was a stage in a longer move from oral evidence to written documents, a change in which the development of wills also contributed greatly. *Domesday Book* was to be referred to by Prince Albert, husband of Queen Victoria and a keen moderniser, in 1859 in his opening address to the annual meeting of the British Association for the Advancement of Science.

A new Church order was also imposed. The Archbishop of Canterbury was removed and replaced by Lanfranc, a key adviser to William. The impact of such discontinuities, however, was lessened by a concern with the institutional interests of churches and monasteries, just as, on the land, intermarriage with English families created new links. There was also a degree of cultural continuity in the state. For example, Lanfranc commissioned from the monk Osbern of Canterbury, a life of St Alphege (Aelfheah), killed by the Danes in 1012. Royal government also looked back to the English state, and the conventions of the latter were more important than a stress on new developments would suggest.

In contrast to the suppression of English opposition, rivalry within the Norman élite led to much instability. This rivalry reflected competition between nobles, disputes between them and the monarchs and, most seriously, dynastic disputes, especially the civil war during the reign of King Stephen (r. 1135–54). At the same time, helped by a widespread desire for cohesion, powerful kings, able to command the respect of the nobles, could suppress and overawe opposition and provide firm government. This was true of William I, of his second son, William II (r. 1087–1100) who succeeded him on the English throne (while the eldest, Robert, became Duke of Normandy), and of William I's youngest son, Henry I (r. 1100–35). All three devoted much of their energy to defending and strengthening their territorial interests in France, Henry defeating Robert in 1106 at Tinchebrai in Normandy to re-unite England and Normandy.

The kings of England also sought greater power in Britain, both seeking to consolidate their control of the North of England and also trying to increase their influence in Scotland and, even more, Wales. William II, who was very much a warrior king, conquered the area of Carlisle. He was subsequently killed in the New Forest by an arrow, possibly a hunting accident but possibly murder.

Although in 1072 William I led an army north and forced Malcolm III of Scotland to do homage for Lothian, Scotland remained independent. There was no Norman conquest of Scotland, but rather a process of Normanisation sponsored by capable kings, especially David I (r. 1124–53). They encouraged the immigration of Norman nobles; and the Norman military machine of knights and castles served as the basis for an extension of royal authority. David minted the first Scottish coins and organised the central government on the Anglo-Norman pattern. Scotland shared with the rest of Britain in a period of substantial demographic and economic growth, which financed the spread of Christian institutions, the development of states and the pursuit of their wars.

An important episode of governmental development occurred under Henry I (r. 1100–35). An expansion of royal judicial activity was matched by the growth of the Exchequer, which provided a regular and methodical collection of royal revenues and control of expenditure. Written records became more common, which was important to the development and consistency of government, and to its need for a permanent base. These processes owed much to the establishment of coherent groups of professional administrators. These *curiales* (men of the Court) were mostly 'new men' who were resented by better-born nobles. This was the social politics repeatedly associated with the quest for more effective and stronger government and with new institutions.

Wars involved struggles for control within Britain, with the kings of Scotland trying to expand their power into the Highlands, Galloway and the Isles, and their counterparts in England doing the same in Wales. There was also the quest for greater territory and control in France, where the interests of the Norman rulers of England were expanded from 1154, when Henry II, grandson of Henry I and the first of the Angevin dynasty (the rulers of Anjou in France) to rule in England, came to the throne. His claim came through the marriage of Henry I's daughter, Matilda, into the House of Anjou. She was the only surviving child of Henry, as the result of the death of his son in a shipwreck in the English Channel. However, her claim to succeed him had been opposed by Stephen (r. 1135–54), the son of William I's daughter, leading to a bitter civil war. Although Matilda captured Stephen at the battle of Lincoln in 1141, neither side was able to win a lasting victory and in parts of the country there was a degree of anarchy as royal government collapsed. This war was finally settled in 1153 by Stephen accepting the succession, after his own death, of Henry II, Matilda's son.

Conflict, abroad and within Britain, led to heavy costs for the Crown. The attempt to meet these accentuated a central tension affecting law and government: that between royal will and regular procedures. These costs were crucial to the problem-driven nature of governmental policy and development. The role of problems was generally more significant than that of particular reform ideas.

Meanwhile, a sense of Anglo-Norman identity and continuity was consciously developed in the twelfth century, with Englishness and Britishness now being seen not in a negative light, but, rather, as memorable bases for a glorious present. The historical perspective was in large part constructed by clerics who had personal links with Anglo-Saxon England. Symeon of Durham, who probably came to the church there from France in 1091, produced a *Tract on the Origins and Progress of this the Church of Durham*, which emphasised Anglo-Saxon roots and looked back to writers of that period, such as Bede. Ailred (*c.* 1109–66), son of a Hexham priest, and successively abbot of the new Cistercian monasteries of Revesby and Rievaulx, composed both a eulogy of Bede's subject, the great Northumbrian holy man, St Cuthbert – whose remains were translated (formally disinterred and removed) into the bold new Norman cathedral at Durham in 1104 – and a life of Edward the Confessor, England's only saint-king, whose body was ceremoniously translated to Westminster in 1163.

The cult of saints, like the emphasis on monastic and ecclesiastical history, necessarily looked to the Anglo-Saxon past. The Church offered not only membership in an international order and a national structure of dioceses, archdeaconries and parishes but also a means for developing local and national senses of identity. Among the historians, Eadmer of Canterbury and John of Worcester were of English origin, while Orderic Vitalis and William of Malmesbury were half-English.

By the early twelfth century, a measure of celebration of the pre-Norman past was in order and this celebration emphasised an English identity separate to that of the king's trans-Channel possessions. In the work of Geoffrey of Monmouth (d. *c.* 1155), Anglo-Norman England latched on to a British past, as his *Historia Regum Britanniae* (*c.* 1136) traced events from the legendary founding of Britain by Aeneas of Troy's grandson, Brutus, and greatly developed the Arthurian legend: Arthur's father was now said to be a descendant of Constantine and a conqueror of the French and the Romans.

Thanks to acquiring territories in France as well as establishing his power in Ireland, Henry II (r. 1154–89) ruled a state more extensive than that of any of his predecessors bar Cnut. Under Henry, the processes of government became less dependent on the personal intervention of the monarch. Furthermore, the enforcement of justice and the collection of royal revenues were improved. Both were royal initiatives, expressed in institutional form, with law and order enforced by royal justices itinerant (travelling around the country). The Common Law gained in strength, helping to consolidate England as a remarkably homogenous state by European standards. An emphasis on the law served as a way to enhance public power, and contributed greatly to the extent to which England was much governed. Lords exercised much of their influence through the public courts system of hundred and shire that was an inheritance from the Old English monarchy, rather than through private judicial power. This was an important source of political, geographical and social cohesion, and helped ensure that influence over the government, rather than defiance of it, was a key dynamic of politics.

As a reminder that more than one explanation is generally appropriate, the focus of Henry II and other monarchs on their territorial position in France needs also to be borne in mind. The people of England had to pay much of the bill and, also, to deal with the consequences of an absent monarch. As a result, while royal powers were put into commission to cope with the absence of successive kings, the administrative development of the Old English state was resumed and, in particular, government remained public to a far greater extent than in France. While France was little more than a confederacy of princely courts, with that of the king the first among equals, England had not fragmented.

The law in England was also an alternative to the settlement of disputes through feuds, and was thus crucial to the attempt by the Crown to monopolise violence and to force public justice on private disputes. Royal authority, which favoured control and punishment, took precedence. Law and justice were both definitions and means of government. This was both a long-term process and a response to the anarchy of Stephen's reign (1135–54) and also to the reality of a society in which vengeance and violence were key attitudes and means. Law brought the central government and the localities closer together, and made the application of justice routine and professional. The role of the localities was enhanced from the mid-1160s as more accusations were brought by local juries rather than royal officials. The common law, with its emphasis on the jury, emerged, as a result, as a product that jointly benefited Crown and society.

Henry II's quarrel with Thomas Becket, a favourite who became Archbishop of Canterbury only to fall victim to royal wrath, reflected the King's resolve to defend governmental interests against the Church. Becket, in contrast, was determined to protect the judicial position of clerics, not least the right of appeals to the Papal Court, an issue that was to resonate down to the Protestant Reformation in the sixteenth century. Henry's angry words led four of his knights to kill Becket in his cathedral in 1170. This shocked Christendom. Becket was memorialised with sainthood in 1173, and his cult both enhanced Canterbury and led to the production of an associated hagiography. The relevant writers, notably Benedict and William of Canterbury, reflect the extent to which the past was shaped to suit the wishes of the present. Becket became a very popular saint, and his tomb was soon the focus for pilgrims. The long appeal of this pilgrimage was to be recorded by Geoffrey Chaucer in his *Canterbury Tales* (*c*. 1387 and later). William I of Scotland, later known as 'the Lion' (r. 1165–1214), was buried in Arbroath Abbey, which he had founded in honour of Becket. Becket also represented the sanctity of opposing tyranny, an idea that could be applied to English politics.

Henry's quarrel with Becket ironically demonstrated not only the struggle of competing authorities but also the tension between bureaucratic processes and individual wilfulness. These processes became more significant as a result of the production and retention of information. Regular record-keeping was seen with the Exchequer Pipe Rolls from the mid-twelfth century and the Close and Patent Rolls of the Chancery from just after 1200. Records of royal and manorial courts were increasingly preserved from the thirteenth century onwards. Tax lists provided data, but compiling them posed problems for government that had to be overcome. For example, the grouping of settlements into vills was important to tax assessment in the fourteenth century. Although bureaucratic practices of government took a while to develop, these practices became more fixed and significant. The governmental structures of the sixteenth century, the period of the so-called 'Tudor Revolution in Government', looked back to the Middle Ages.

The thirteenth and fourteenth centuries

Alongside the stress on law and justice, the Crown could also be very arbitrary, and the greater coercive power of government made it a formidable instrument of tyranny. This was an issue under the bullying Henry II and also helps explain the immense resentment aroused by his son King John (r. 1199–1216), who was tough, nasty and, crucially, unsuccessful. He lacked the charisma, not least military prowess, of his elder brother, Richard I (r. 1189–99), the Lionheart, who had played an active role on the Third Crusade, a powerful instance of England's participation in the wider Christian community. Richard played a key part in capturing Acre (in modern Israel) from the Islamic leader Saladin, and also defeated the latter in battle; but Jerusalem, which Saladin had conquered, eluded his grasp.

Captured returning from the Third Crusade, Richard was held to ransom by the Holy Roman Empire. The resulting harsh tax assessment, a quarter of the value of all religious and secular property, led in London in 1196 to opposition by the city's poor, led by William Fitz Osbert. Richard's Justiciar, Hubert Walter, felt he had to act and besieged Fitz Osbert in the sanctuary of St Mary-le-Bow on Cheapside in London. Fitz Osbert and nine followers were hanged.

John's epithet 'Softsword' summed up his lack of a good reputation. His failure abroad, which included, in 1204, the conquest of Normandy by Philip Augustus of France, a major blow to royal prestige and finances, helped to encourage John's domestic opponents to rise in rebellion. In 1215, John was forced to accept the terms of what was later to be called Magna Carta. This charter of liberties was a condemnation of John's use of feudal, judicial and other governmental powers, for it defined and limited royal rights. Magna Carta was in effect an enormous list of everything that was wrong with government as John had applied it, notably arbitrary royal action that offended the idea and practice of justice. In response, in the Charter, baronial liberties were protected and freemen were provided with some guarantees against arbitrary royal actions. The Crown was not to be able to determine its rights alone, and, instead, Magna Carta asserted the importance of placing royal power under the law.

What happened at Runnymede near Windsor on 15 June 1215 was a peacemaking ceremony that established a new political dispensation and a new legal framework for the exercise of monarchy. The charter was in effect England's first written constitution, creating a new relationship between the king and the law. It settled the point that the king was under the law. Clause 40 affirmed that no-one could sell, deny or delay justice. As a result, Magna Carta was to acquire totemic significance, being seen as the key constitutional document and settlement in English history and being cited by opponents of what was presented as arbitrary governmental power, notably in the thirteenth and seventeenth centuries.

The principle of placing royal authority under the law was followed up under John's son and successor, Henry III (r. 1216–72). His minority (1216–27) was significant in grounding the idea of consent to the actions of government. Magna Carta became embedded in the law during this minority: not, in fact, the 1215 original, but the version of 1217 (when it got its name) which was reissued in 1225. What originally had been an opposition document forced on John, was shredded of its most offensive clauses, most of which were specific to John, and reissued as the new king's free gift. Once his minority was over, Henry's prestige was affected by failure in war in France, while he was unpopular as a result of what was seen as misgovernment, not least the influence allowed to royal favourites.

In order to enforce what they regarded as good kingship, many of the barons, instead, sought to take power out of Henry's hands. In 1258, a baronial group wrested control of the government and pushed through reforms to its workings designed in particular to curb royal abuses. These reforms, known as the Provisions of Oxford, were intended to unite society. The baronial council was to be responsible to Parliament, while the reform proposals were proclaimed in 1258 in English as well as French and Latin.

Rivalries among the baronial reformers provided Henry with an opportunity to regain power, which he had done by 1261. However, Simon de Montfort refused to accept this situation and, in 1263, rebelled at the head of a baronial faction that was determined to restore the Provisions. He took control of London but was unable to prevent civil war, which broke out in 1264. The baronial army defeated and captured Henry III at Lewes. In turn, however, de Montfort was defeated at Evesham in 1265 by Henry's son, the future Edward I. De Montfort was killed in the battle. Henry was restored.

The Scottish monarchs were more successful in defending their interests without civil war and constitutional struggles. Furthermore, they spread their power out from the central lowlands, extending their control in Galloway, Moray, Argyll, Ross, Caithness and the Western Isles, from the late twelfth to the late thirteenth century. Broader social, economic and cultural developments also contributed to a measure of cohesion. The notion of Scotland became stronger as patterns of behaviour associated with the royal heartland spread into other areas. Furthermore, the formation of a distinctively Scottish Church contributed to a developing sense of national identity.

Alexander II (r. 1214–49) allied with the barons opposed to John and they recognised Scottish claims to Northumberland, Cumberland and Westmorland, a claim accepted by Prince Louis of France who contested the English succession with Henry III. In 1216, Alexander marched as far south as Dover. However, the defeat of a rebel-French army at Lincoln in 1217 not only led to the consolidation of Henry's authority and the end of the French attempt but also undermined Alexander. In December 1217, he made peace and surrendered his claims. This was confirmed by the Quitclaim or Treaty of York in 1237. Alexander focused in the 1220s and 1230s on campaigning within Scotland, extending royal control in Argyll, Ross, Caithness and Galloway.

Under Alexander III (r. 1249–86), the power of the Canmore dynasty of kings of Scotland reached its zenith, but dynastic mischance ensured his succession by a three-year-old, Margaret, the Maid of Norway. Edward I of England (r. 1272–1307), who had already conquered north Wales in 1277–82, ending its independence, saw this as a dynastic opportunity, able to settle political issues. In 1289, by the Treaty of Salisbury, Margaret's marriage to the future Edward II was agreed. The rights and laws of Scotland were to be preserved, but, in essence, the treaty prefigured the union of the Crowns that was to occur in 1603. Margaret, however, died in 1290.

Edward I's subsequent attempt to dominate Scotland eventually met with resistance when his choice as King, John Balliol, turned against him. A natural authoritarian, Edward was also concerned that an independent Scotland would support his French rival. This resistance was defeated in 1296 and (after a rebellion by William Wallace, who won a major victory at Stirling in 1297) at the battle of Falkirk in 1298. However, Robert Bruce, grandson of a claimant to the throne in 1291–2, rebelled in 1306 and was crowned as Robert I (r. 1306–29). Initially, the forces of Edward I retained the initiative, but Edward II (r. 1307–27) did not focus on Scotland and Robert was able to conquer much of it. In 1314, Bruce routed Edward II at Bannockburn outside Stirling. The major frontier fortress of Berwick fell to the Scots in 1318.

Scottish independence was asserted anew by the Declaration of Arbroath of 1320, a letter to the Pope proclaiming the ancient independence of Scotland. This letter is quoted in the entrance to the new national museum in Edinburgh, a museum that underplays the British dimension to Scottish history. In 1328, by the Treaty of Northampton–Edinburgh, Scottish independence and Bruce's kingship were recognised.

These outcomes were rapidly challenged by Edward III and Edward Balliol. Balliol, a claimant to the Scottish throne, gained power there in 1332, and again in 1333, at the expense of the young David II (r. 1329–71). In 1334, Balliol performed homage for his kingdom to Edward III (r. 1327–77), who had provided crucial military support in 1333. However, Balliol was unable to maintain his control, and David returned from refuge in France in 1341.

The struggle in Scotland was subsumed into, and, in part, super- seded by, that with France, as success in the early stages of what became known as the Hundred Years' War led Edward III to assert, from 1340 onwards, a claim to the French throne. This claim reflected the opportunity provided by dynastic change in France, but took further the pursuit of the claim to regain territories ruled by Edward's Angevin predecessors, notably Henry II. Despite major victories at Crécy (1346) and Poiters (1356) by English armies, which owed much to the firepower of their longbowmen, Edward found the conflict intractable. Similarly, victory over the invading David II of Scotland at Neville's Cross near Durham in 1346 did not bring control over Scotland even though David, who had intervened on the French side, was imprisoned by the English until 1357.

Edward's attempt to stabilise his gains in France by a treaty in 1360 (the Peace of Brétigny) failed, and war resumed in 1369. By 1375, he retained little more than several coastal bases, principally Calais (captured in 1347 after a siege) and also positions in south- west France.

The costs of conflict, particularly when unsuccessful, accen- tuated disputes between rulers and nobles, many of which reflected tension over royal patronage. This was particularly the case with Edward II, a lacklustre monarch who failed to command confidence and mishandled patronage, alienating much of the nobility. There was a major political crisis in England in 1297, in which many nobles resisted Edward I's demands for high war taxation, while in 1311 Edward II was forced to accept Ordinances restricting his power. His favourite, Piers Gaveston, who much irritated the nobility, was executed by the barons in 1312. In 1318, the dispute between Edward and the nobles, under his powerful cousin Thomas, Earl of Lancaster, was temporarily settled by the Treaty of Leake. A council was imposed to Edward. In 1319, there was fresh failure at the hands of the Scots and in 1321 civil war broke out over the ambitions of the Despensers, a father and son who supported Edward. Lancaster initially succeeded, but, in 1322, Edward's power revived and Lancaster was defeated at Boroughbridge and later executed.

Subsequent failure against Scotland and France exacerbated an unpopularity stemming from a bullying and exacting government. In 1326, Edward's alienated wife, Isabella, invaded with the support of the Count of Hainault in the Low Countries. The government collapsed. Edward was captured and his supporters executed.

In January 1327, Edward II was removed from the throne in Parliament, being murdered in Berkeley Castle soon after. This was not restraint of royal government on the pattern of Magna Carta. Indeed, the killing of Edward II was a testimony to the failure of thirteenth-century attempts to restrain the king. English kingship had proved too powerful to restrain in this fashion. Control of a different kind failed in 1330 when Edward III overthrew his mother Isabella and her lover Roger Mortimer, Earl of March. She was detained, he was executed after trial in Parliament.

Although Edward III was stronger, more successful and more popular than Edward II, mounting criticism of his government in the later, more difficult, years of his reign, culminated, in the Good Parliament (1376), in attacks on government corruption and in the rejection of tax demands. In Scotland, in turn, David II faced successful opposition by hostile nobles led by Robert Stewart, later King, as Robert II.

The development of Parliaments, in both England and Scotland, reflected the sense of the need for a political body that would serve, however episodically, as a national political focus. This need was the product of the greater appeal of the national, rather than regional, sense of political identity. In England, the development of Parliament, which was part of the delicate political compact necessary for peace and stability, entailed the broadening out of what had originated as the king's council of barons.

Parliament was not mentioned in Magna Carta, indeed not until the 1230s, but Magna Carta was a stage in the development of Parliament, which turned out to be a pathway to constitutional government that was more effective than the issuing of charters by a monarch. Clauses twelve and fourteen of Magna Carta were particularly significant. Clause twelve established that no scutage (money in lieu of military service) or aid (tax) could be levied without common counsel, an idea which looked back to the Roman Law maxim that what touches all should be approved by all. Clause fourteen established that this was to be obtained from the greater tenants in chief and from lesser tenants in chief who were to be summoned via sheriffs. In practice, these clauses meant no taxation without representation. They were left out in the reissues, but the idea of consent was now very much to become part of the political system.

Under Henry III, shire knights began to be elected to Parliament, and from 1265 selected towns sent representatives. The new concept of representation was outlined in the writs summoning representatives of the clergy, counties and boroughs to the 1295 Parliament: they were instructed to appear with authority to give advice and consent on behalf of the communities they represented. In contrast, the nobles appeared on their own behalf.

During the fourteenth century, the role of Parliament expanded, in large part due to the need to raise taxation for warfare. The long wars with France and Scotland, and the size of the armies deployed, including over 30,000 men at Crécy, meant that more taxation than ever before was required. Taxes were justified as being for the 'common good'. This was part of a long pattern in English, later British, history: the poverty of the state in light of its extensive demands and the resulting need for parliamentary approval of taxes and loans. The need for taxation was traded against the demand for redress of grievances and for the entrenching of individual liberty. Thus, the Statute of Purveyors of 1362 saw the regularising by law of what had been a royal abuse, the compulsory purchase of supplies. Similarly, in 1679, the Habeas Corpus Act regulated detention pending trial. As a result, the constitution and the establishment of rights became a matter of the assertion of parliamentary sovereignty and not basic law, as in many other states. This emphasis on the sovereignty of Parliament, a body that could revise its decisions, ensured that the constitution was regarded as incremental and seamless, and not based on a founding document as in America. Indeed, America very much looked back to Magna Carta. The common lawyers, such as Sir Edward Coke, who had played a major role in discovering a new political role for Magna Carta in the early seventeenth century, were heavily involved in drafting the charters of the English colonies established in North America. The rejection of George III in 1775–83 was seen as another instance of the opposition to John. Similarly in Scotland, Parliament developed from the king's council of bishops and earls, and borough representatives gained regular access.

National identity was encouraged not only by the development of Parliaments but also of historical accounts in both England and Scotland. Those in Scotland emphasised distinctiveness from England and focused on the struggle for independence. Conflict also played a role in developing national identity in England, but it was not the sole factor. The Norman monarchs sought to claim the historical inheritance of Old English kingship, in part by ecclesiastical patronage. This was taken forward by the sponsorship of historical writing. Later kings, particularly Henry III and Edward III, very much supported such activity and added fresh initiatives of their own.

Edward III used the Arthurian legend to add the authority of age to his embrace of chivalric ideas. This was seen with the establishment of the Order of the Garter in 1348–9 and the foundation of the College of St George to serve the royal chapel in Windsor Castle. This chapel was re-dedicated to St George whom Edward chose as the patron saint for the Order. This linkage of saint and nation was intended to bring prestige and success, and, in some circumstances, can be seen as akin to a form of white magic.

A different aspect of national identity was provided by the expulsion of England's Jewish community by Edward I in 1290. A Jewish community, possibly immigrants from Rouen in Normandy was in place in 1130. The role of the Jews in helping to finance the Crown and other leading figures led, however, to growing criticism. This had a violent consequence, with massacres in London in 1189 and York in 1190. Thereafter, public hostility to Jews became more conspicuous. A change in policy only occurred under Oliver Cromwell in the 1650s.

In Scotland, a sense of separate identity was powerfully affirmed by writers keen to show that Scotland was a distinct state with its own history. John Barbour's poem the *Brus*, composed in Scots in 1375, was a national epic centring on Robert the Bruce. It was followed in the 1380s by John Fordun's *Chronicle of the Scottish People*.

A stress on proto-nationalism, Parliament and national politics provides a modern tone to this period, one particularly characterised by ideas and terms of development and progress. This approach captures an important aspect of change, but also underplays other themes, notably the major role of the Church, a role that had its own capacity for development.

The Church very much represented an international identity. Moreover, a series of ecclesiastical developments enhanced this. The rise of the international (French-led) monastic orders of Cluny and Cîteaux was important. So also was the rise, in the twelfth century, of the papally directed, Continentally shaped, canon law. This was linked to the decline of English Church Councils in the face of Continental ones for the entire Church. The English and, later, Scottish universities were part of an international intellectual development. Stephen Langton, Archbishop of Canterbury from 1207 until 1228, studied and taught at the University of Paris. He played a key role in the negotiations leading to Magna Carta, and the charter reflected his Biblical commentaries on the bad kings of the Old Testament.

A vivid reminder of the mindset linked to the Church is provided by the Hereford *mappa mundi* (world map), a copy, which is on display in Hereford, of the map made in about 1290–1300 of one that the cleric Richard Haldingham (d. 1278) had produced there. This map has Christ sitting in Majesty on the Day of Judgment at its apex outside the frame. Christ in Majesty was a certainty above a Creation, the goal and nature of which were clear in God's purpose, but which man could only partly fathom. As the symbol of Creation, the circle acted to contain the ephemeral nature of human activity. The use of Anglo-Norman as well as Latin in the map indicates that the information offered was for laity as well as clergy. This was a Britain in which faith was also registered in the churches that covered the land. New monastic and preaching orders were possibly as significant for the experience of the people as the doings of kings.

Alongside an emphasis on change, it is necessary to think of a still-rural Britain where travel, especially by land, was difficult (so that coastal transport was far quicker and more common), where the problems of distance kept most people for most of the time in their own neighbourhoods, and where the dark, the damp and the cold pressed hard on people.

Topography as well as hardship and anxiety exaggerated the impact of distance. This helped ensure that, although about 30–40 per cent of all grain grown was marketed by the thirteenth century, there was a greater need for all-round agricultural production than was to be the case by the late nineteenth century, or, still more, today. Thus, the detailed pattern of land-use was far more complex and interdependent than might be suggested by references to upland pasture and lowland arable. In upland areas, grain was grown in small quantities as a subsistence crop, accentuating the difficult nature of agriculture. Pasture areas were characterised by dispersed settlement, frequently in the form of isolated farmsteads, while arable regions were more populated and had nucleated (village) settlements.

At the level of the individual farmstead, and again of the village, there was a degree of self-reliance that is totally alien to modern farmers. This self-reliance reflected the relative difficulty of preservation and transport in an age before refrigeration and motor vehicles, but also the intensity of very local systems of exchange, as well as the degree to which self- and local-reliance made more economic sense than in the modern age of specialisation through comparative profit margins.

The economic environment became far less benign in the fourteenth century. As with many developments on this scale, notably in agriculture and demography, this was part of a far wider change. Across Europe, the long period of demographic (population) and economic expansion that had underpinned social development since the tenth century, and that had led to a marked extension of farmed land at the expense of woods, marshes and heaths, came to an end. Population growth had resulted in demand-led economic activity and an expansion of the social fabric: new towns, villages, roads, bridges and markets.

This process was seen in both England and Scotland, and was linked to the spread of the money economy. There was a marked rise in the amount of money in circulation in the thirteenth century, and it has been argued that 20 times as much money was in circulation by 1300 as in 1100. Monetarisation aided trade, facilitated credit, and encouraged a sense of economic opportunity and social fluidity. In the shape of monasteries clearing the unfarmed 'waste' and producing goods for sale – notably wool from the Cistercian abbeys, such as Fountains and Tintern – the Church was also an important cause of change. There was a significant rise in English wool exports from the twelfth century. The new tax valuations required for the lay subsidy of 1334 indicate that the five wealthiest English counties per square mile were, in descending order, Middlesex, Oxfordshire, Norfolk, Bedfordshire and Berkshire, all of which were in the South-East.

Across England from the very late twelfth century, fords at major crossing points were replaced by bridges, which increasingly rested on stone arches and were able to accommodate carts. A developing network of regular carriers' routes was instrumental in creating a national transport system. Mercantile credit was crucial to this system.

Economic growth and demographic expansion came to an end, however. This was most dramatically the case with the Black Death, an epidemic, probably of bubonic plague, which killed about a third of the English population between 1348 and 1351, seriously disrupted the economy and public finances, and probably contributed to a loss of confidence in the benign nature of life. Scotland and Wales were hit from 1349, although, being less densely populated, they may have suffered less seriously. Like the Great Famine of 1315–17 caused by harvest failure resulting from bad weather, the plague hit population levels that were anyhow under pressure as a result of the impact of earlier expansion on resources: population growth had outstripped agricultural expansion. Later plague attacks followed in 1361, 1369, 1375 and subsequently. The population of London (including Southwark and Westminster) may have been halved, to about 40,000, by the 1370s.

The Black Death also helped make labour relations more volatile, by leading to attempts to control labour, which was now scarcer. These attempts accentuated strains in rural society that were heightened by a poll tax designed to fund the unsuccessful war with France. These strains culminated in 1381 in the Peasants' Revolt, or, more properly, the Great Revolt, as the rebels were not all peasants: there was a strong urban element. Alongside hardship, a cause of the revolt was the rising expectations of the lower orders coming into collision with the repressive policies of the government and landed classes. Indeed, Froissart commented on the affluence of the English lower orders, arguing that the cause of the revolt was 'the ease and riches that the English people' had.

The revolt involved risings across much of England, but disorder focused on the capital. Demonstrating peasants occupied London, seizing the Tower of London and killing unpopular ministers, notably Simon of Sudbury, the Archbishop of Canterbury and Chancellor, who was responsible for the unpopular poll tax. Seeking the abolition of serfdom and also targeting foreigners, the rebels did not wish to create a new governmental system, but rather to pressure the young Richard II (r. 1377–99) into changes of policy that would accord with their concept of good kingship.

On 15 June 1381, as the crisis continued, Richard met the main body of the rebels under Wat Tyler at Smithfield, just outside the walls of London. During the meeting, William Walworth, Mayor of London, believing that Tyler was threatening Richard, lunged forward and stabbed him in the neck, whereupon one of the king's knights despatched him with a sword through the stomach. Astutely, Richard averted further violence by promising to be the rebels' leader. The peasants returned home. Richard revoked his promise and the surviving leaders were then hunted down. The rising had shown a depth of popular alienation, one that was not matched in Scotland.

Richard II survived the Peasants' Revolt, but he faced opposition from the lords who had dominated his minority. Richard's attempts to overcome this opposition helped lead to a violent and unstable politics that was accentuated by his authoritarian tendencies. The mismatch between the appearance and substance of power under Richard was exacerbated by a loss of prestige due to failure in the war with France. Richard's problems culminated in 1399 when he was seized and forced to abdicate by a rebellious cousin he had disinherited, Henry Bolingbroke, who became Henry IV (r. 1399–1413).

This coup reflected the dynastic and political problems that were to be created from rivalries between the numerous descendants of Edward III. The Dukes of Lancaster and York were the key cadet (junior) lines of the ruling house, Richard II being the son of Edward's eldest son. The latter, Edward, 'The Black Prince', the victor of the battle of Poitiers over the French in 1356, predeceased his long-lived father. In 1400, the imprisoned Richard was killed in Pontefract Castle where he had been imprisoned, in order to remove a rallying point for opposition to the new Lancastrian dynasty.

The fourteenth century therefore closed in crisis. Demographic and economic difficulties led to rural depopulation in the shape of deserted and shrunken villages, the remains of some of which can still be seen. This was a change to rural society greater than those which arose from eighteenth-century enclosure, the impact of global competition in food production in the late nineteenth century, or the large-scale mechanisation in the second half of the twentieth. This change was also more significant since rural society was, in relative terms, more important economically and demographically than it was during later periods.

Furthermore, in the 1390s and 1400s, Richard II was unsuccessful in France, there was a major rising in Wales against English rule, that of Owain Glyndwr (Owen Glendower), in 1400, while two rival factions within the Scottish royal family competed for control. Moreover, in England, the Lollard movement inspired by the radical theologian John Wycliff (also given as Wycliffe *c.* 1329–84) challenged the position of Pope and priests and led to the disturbing reality of heresy. In 1381, Wycliff, who had criticised Eucharistic doctrine, was condemned. There was an unsuccessful Lollard rising under Sir John Oldcastle in 1414. Emphasising the authority of the Bible, not the Church, Lollardy looked towards Protestant activity in London, Kent and Norfolk in the early sixteenth century.

There were contrary strengths, however. In the case of religion, the large number of parishes helped to ensure a detailed pattern of belonging, with the churches serving as the centres of identity for particular neighbourhoods. This sense of local identity, ringing out with church bells, and maintained by frequent processions, linked the generations, as parish churches were the venue for weddings, baptisms and burials. The memory represented by a sense of family coherence focused upon churches. The importance of this role helps to explain the disruption caused by the Protestant Reformation in the sixteenth century.

Moreover, there were strengths in government and the broader political culture. The greater sophistication of royal administration ensured that records that were subsequently to be used by historians became more plentiful. Alongside the Hereford *mappa mundi*, and suggesting different concerns, there is the Gough Map, a practical map of Britain of about 1375, possibly produced for administrative uses. It provided an effective route map and showed nearly 3,000 miles of road. As a different form of record, there were developments in timekeeping. Richard of Wallingford, Abbot of St Albans (1327–34) improved the weight-driven clock with features such as a double-pallet escapement. His St Albans clock also had one of the earliest hour-striking mechanisms.

The growth of cloth exports was vital to transport developments, to the trade balance and to government finances. The development of Parliament offered a political and governmental forum and tool, treating England as a whole.

The rise of vernacular culture in England had already seen William Langland's *Piers Plowman* (1362–92) and Geoffrey Chaucer's *Canterbury Tales* (*c.* 1387 and later). The son of a vintner, Chaucer (*c.* 1343–1400) became Comptroller of the Customs for the port of London in 1374 and Clerk of the King's Works in 1389, overseeing the building of the wharf at the Tower of London. There were Scottish equivalents, notably John Barbour.

Vernacular usage represented a rejection of the French-speaking culture that had arrived with the Norman Conquest. The role of Latin and of Anglo-Norman or Norman-French (the French of England) declined. Vernacular usage, which was encouraged by the adoption of English by government agencies, for example for proceedings in the London Sheriffs' courts in 1356, offered a degree of social unity that could underlie political action across social divides. Such action was to be significant in the rejection of authority, lay and ecclesiastical, that was regarded as unacceptable, whether it was bad monarchs or unwelcome Church practices. Lollardy favoured an English Bible.

It was far from clear in 1400 that England would feature as a major power or as a model of political progress. That France was also bitterly divided between two aristocratic factions with dynastic links to the monarch did not make the situation in England and Scotland better, but it did indicate a more general precariousness. The contrast between the limitations of Western Europe and the major states of Asia, notably Ming China, was readily apparent to the few Western travellers who got there.

CHAPTER THREE

1400–1750

In 1400, the deposed Richard II of England was murdered in Pontefract Castle. In 1746, the Scottish army raised in support of the Jacobite (exiled Stuart) cause was destroyed by regular government forces at the battle of Culloden east of Inverness. It is all too easy, in a short chapter, to allow civil war to crowd out the picture. Indeed, the English Wars of the Roses and Scottish dynastic/aristocratic conflicts in the fifteenth century, and struggles across Britain linked to religion in the sixteenth, were followed by the civil wars of 1638–52 across Britain. Then came what we might call the War of the British Succession, most of which was fought in Ireland and Scotland. This conflict began when the Protestant Dukes of Monmouth and Argyll sought to overthrow James II and VII (II of England and VII of Scotland) in 1685, Monmouth, an illegitimate son of Charles II, claiming the succession, only to be defeated at Sedgemoor. The war, which went through very different separate stages, culminated in the defeat at Culloden of James II and VII's grandson, Bonnie Prince Charlie, Charles Edward Stuart, by William, Duke of Cumberland, the second son of George II.

These conflicts are properly to the fore in any political account, for they serve to underline the uncertainty of developments. The fate of battle is, by its nature, far from inevitable, while the fact of civil war highlighted the consequences of political division and, frequently, of a lack of calibre, or at least luck, in royal leadership. Wars also interacted with some of the major long-term themes in British history, such as the frequent dominance of southern England and the restriction of royal power. Conversely, the use of long-term is problematic: different verdicts in war, notably in the rebellions against the Reformation, the mid-seventeenth century civil wars, and the War of the British Succession in 1688–1746, might well have qualified or cut short these themes.

This use of the counterfactual or 'what if?' theme may irritate when there is only so much space for discussing what actually happened. However, the possibilities of what might have been, in so far as they were considered in the past, proved part of this history. Moreover, a determination to prevent outcomes that appeared possible helped drive much government policy, whether the imprisonment and execution of potential focal points of rebellion, as under Henry VIII (r. 1509–47), the organisation of a spy system designed to thwart conspiracies, as under Elizabeth I (r. 1558–1603), or military preparations.

It is also important to note the wider international dimension. A focus on whether history should be English, British or four nations (English, Irish, Scottish, Welsh), can lead to a failure to connect with the extent to which it is appropriate to consider issues at the European and global levels. The European level was certainly the case for two of the most important changes in Britain: the Protestant Reformation, and the development of trans-oceanic trade and colonisation. Britain was at the forefront of neither change. Both, however, became crucial to British interests and identity, and helped to define Britain until the late twentieth century. Although this definition has in large part been lost in a changing Britain, the consequences of the Reformation and of overseas expansion remain important, not least in the contours of British public culture and in Britain's links with the trans-oceanic world.

War with France

In light of these important changes in the sixteenth century, it is very easy to rush through the fifteenth. It was a period of economic stagnation, acute political division and religious stasis, or at least of less economic and religious change than in the Tudor age that followed. Much of the importance of the fifteenth century, indeed, was that of failure, particularly, posthumously, that of

Henry V (r. 1413–22), a warrior prince and then king, who sought to revive the claim of his great-grandfather, Edward III, to the French throne. Henry had no sense that the Channel should act as a boundary to his authority. Although identifying with the cult of St George, and presented essentially as an assertor of Englishness in Shakespeare's play *Henry V* (1599), the king himself followed all his predecessors since William I in envisaging a realm that spanned the English Channel. Normandy seemed closer to his centre of power in southern England than the margins of his possessions in the British Isles, and was also a more attractive prospect for operations and expansion. There was also the sense of a great tradition to be maintained and fame to be gained.

Henry indeed won great glory from his victory at Agincourt on 25 October 1415, a battle in which English and Welsh archers inflicted heavy casualties on the much larger, attacking French army. This victory was followed, two years later, by the start of the conquest of Normandy. Its capital, Rouen, fell in 1419. Weakened by aristocratic disaffection, the weak and defeated Charles VI of France betrothed his daughter, Catherine, to Henry, and, by the Treaty of Troyes of 1420, recognised Henry (and his heirs) as his heir.

Had Henry V lived longer, he might have created a new polity, but asserting control over the whole of France was a formidable task. In the event he died, probably of dysentery, in 1422, leaving an heir less than one year old. Under Henry VI (r. 1422–61, 1470–1), the English were driven out of all bar Calais and the Channel Isles. On behalf of Charles VI's son, Charles VII, Joan of Arc rallied French resistance in the late 1420s, notably at Orleans. Subsequently, English operations ran out of impetus, and John, Duke of Burgundy, a key supporter of the English cause in France, abandoned Henry in 1435. The armies of Charles VII then drove the English out, with defeats at Formigny (1450) and Castillon (1453) sealing the fates of Normandy and Gascony respectively. French cannon played a significant role in both battles.

Although Calais was held until lost by Mary in 1558, the claim to the French throne was only abandoned in the reign of George III, and the Channel Isles, the last of the Norman legacy, are still held by the Crown, France was lost. There were to be further invasions of France, by Edward IV, Henry VII and Henry VIII, but the failure of these rulers to achieve their ambitions in France was important to the development of English nationhood and government and helped underline an insular character to Britain's subsequent European identity. Indeed, the long-term inability to sustain a territorial presence in France provided a backdrop to later trans-oceanic ambitions.

Fifteenth-century divisions

Defeat in France accentuated Henry VI's weaknesses as king, as well as giving the impression of failure, and this failure helped precipitate the Wars of the Roses, the struggle between the houses of Lancaster (the royal line) and York. These wars began with disaffection in the early 1450s about the government, disaffection which spanned aristocratic opposition to royal favouritism as well as the popular hostility shown in Cade's Rebellion (1450). This rebellion reflected the extent to which popular action was part of the wider political world. Deference might be expressed in civic rituals, but it was frequently not shown in practice.

Beginning in Kent, Cade's Rebellion was a product of extortion by manorial officials, as well as widespread hostility to the government. Having defeated a royal army at Sevenoaks, the rebels seized London and killed unpopular officials. However, as in 1381, a royal pardon destroyed the cohesion of the rebels, and Cade, who had lost support in London, was subsequently captured. In the face of the rebellion, Henry VI had run away, an unimpressive response that helped inspire subsequent Yorkist sympathies in the city.

Armed opposition to Henry's favourites led to conflict from 1455 onward with Richard, Duke of York, attacking the lords closest to the King. The dynamics of domestic and military power had changed with the spread of 'Bastard Feudalism', in which lords rewarded their followers, and retained their services, with an annual payment of money, rather than with land. The resulting clientage was dominated by powerful nobles whose willingness to raise troops was crucial to the ability of rulers to field armies. This form of patronage and clientage was not necessarily a cause of civil conflict but, in the event of a breakdown in relations between monarch and nobles, or in the ranks of the latter, it made it easier for the nobles to mobilise and sustain their strength. The extent to which the economy was in serious difficulties accentuated these problems. A loss in silver, much of which had been sent abroad to support the war in France, contributed to a fall in the total currency in circulation.

Henry IV and Henry V had rapidly suppressed opposition to them, Henry IV successfully overcoming the powerful interest of the Percy family, crushing their rebellions in 1403, 1405 and 1408, and Henry V thwarting a conspiracy on the eve of his invasion of France. In contrast, Henry VI was unable to suppress opposition. He was mentally ill and could not cope with crises, and his son and heir, Edward, was an infant. The crisis of the 1450s became a dynastic struggle when Richard, Duke of York, who was the grandson of Edward III's fourth surviving son, claimed the throne in 1460. York was defeated and killed that year at Wakefield. However, his vigorous son seized power as Edward IV in 1461 at the age of 18. Edward confirmed his success by defeating the Lancastrians soon after at Towton in a battle that may have involved as many as 60,000 troops – which would make it the battle with the greatest number of combatants on British soil.

Edward IV was able to suppress continued Lancastrian opposition in the early 1460s in part because the Wars of the Roses were closely linked to the context of international rivalry. French and Burgundian support were the key element. Thus, in 1463, Edward was able to negotiate a truce with Louis XI of France. Louis promised to abandon the Lancastrians and to end the Auld Alliance with Scotland. This led Scotland, later that year, to agree a truce with England. Neither was to support the other's rebels. Scotland abandoned the Lancastrians. The sequel was Lancastrian defeats at Hedgeley Moor and Hexham in 1464, and Henry VI was captured in 1465.

However, the Yorkist interest fractured when Richard, Earl of Warwick, 'the Kingmaker', resenting a loss of influence, rejected his cousin Edward and turned to the Lancastrians. As a result, Edward was overthrown in 1470, with Louis XI of France backing Henry VI's return to the throne.

In 1471, this led Edward to make an alliance with Charles the Bold, Duke of Burgundy, Louis's principal opponent. With his help, and by seizing the initiative, Edward regained the throne through battle, in 1471, defeating Warwick at Barnet and the Lancastrians at Tewkesbury. These battles led to the death of Warwick and of Henry VI's son, Edward; Henry himself was killed in the Tower of

London. Edward IV then ruled with little opposition until he died in 1483.

He was succeeded by his 12-year-old son, Edward V, but the latter swiftly disappeared, probably murdered in the royal apartments in the Tower of London at the behest of his uncle and successor, Richard III (r. 1483–5). Belief in this murder greatly discredited the latter, a violent man.

These frequent changes created a sense of anarchy, seen for example in a revival of fortified features in the houses of the élite. The violent nature of politics was scarcely conducive to good government. The Wars of the Roses, indeed, provided the context for the working out of rivalries between the nobility in the regions – for example in Devon – as had also been the case in the civil war of Stephen's reign (1135–54).

There were also serious problems of disorder in Scotland, although the armies involved in civil conflict were smaller than in England. Scotland faced not only dynastic conflict, with two rival factions within the royal family competing for control from 1384. The Scottish rulers were also confronted with the issue of dominance over extensive peripheral regions to an extent far greater than in England. The latter had already been a major theme in the late twelfth and thirteenth centuries, but, during the wars of independence against England, some powerful magnates, such as the Earls of Douglas in the Borders, had increased their possessions and strength, and this process restricted royal power.

The monarchs had to devote much effort to the task of regaining authority. James I (r. 1406–37), reimposed royal control in the Highlands, executing recalcitrant clan chiefs, but, in 1429 and 1431, he had to campaign against a more formidable opponent, the Lord of the [Western] Isles. This Lordship rose in power in the fourteenth and fifteenth centuries. James II crushed the main branch of the Douglases in 1452–5, James III gained Orkney and the Shetlands in 1472 and Ross in 1476, and in 1493 James IV destroyed the position of the Lords of the Isles and extended his authority to the Hebrides.

Yet, the monarchs still faced a difficult situation. James I was murdered in his bedchamber in an attempted coup in 1437, while James III faced serious aristocratic opposition and, in 1488, unable to muster sufficient support, he was killed shortly after his defeat by rebels at Sauchieburn. The rebels then took over the government, only themselves to face rebellion in 1489.

The period as a whole was one of serious difficulties in Britain because of the strains arising from economic problems. The Black Death was followed not by a recovery in population numbers but by a period of general stagnation, with fresh attacks of plague in 1361–2, 1369 and 1375. This stagnation reduced the market for domestic agriculture and industry, which acted as a general damper on the economy. The fall in population resulted in many deserted or shrunken villages, and the pattern of ridge and furrow that is still visible in modern pastures shows the extent of ploughland that was returned to grazing by animals. The trade at most markets and fairs declined, hitting town life. The long-term context was of a downturn in the climate. As it became colder, so the growing season of crops was limited, which reduced their yield. Scotland suffered disproportionately from climate change.

At the same time, as a reminder of the variety of interests affected by economic trends, the absence of population growth made it possible for peasants to exploit demands for labour, and they were also helped by the decline of serfdom and the resulting increase of fluidity in tenurial relations. Labour-rents were commuted into money payments, and this process increased the penetration of the money economy into the rural world. The higher level of wages allowed workers more leisure time: drinking socially in alehouses became more widespread, and increased legislation against games was prompted by the same trend. The general rise in stock farming meant that meat-eating spread further down the social scale.

Furthermore, the growth of the cloth trade provided Britain with a key economic advantage. Parts of England and Scotland, particularly East Anglia and the Southern Uplands of Scotland, had for long been centres of wool exports, providing the basic raw material for the important cloth industry in the Low Countries. Describing England, John Trevisa in the fourteenth century, in his translation of Higden's *Polychronicon*, noted the presence of sheep bearing 'good wool … Flanders loving the wool of this land'. This agriculturally based industry was particularly important, first because this was an age that did not have synthetic textiles, and, second, because the range of industrial production was more limited than subsequently.

In the fourteenth and fifteenth century, there was a switch from exports of wool to exports of woollen cloth, as its manufacture now took place in Britain. This development brought considerable prosperity that can still be glimpsed in the churches of towns such as Lavenham and Long Melford (both in Suffolk), although the wealth of East Anglia was not matched in the North, while the relative importance of Lincolnshire declined in favour of Norfolk and Suffolk. By the 1540s, about 88 per cent of English cloth exports went through London, enhancing the capital's wealth and political pull.

The cloth trade also provided the Crown with a key source of revenue, and one that required a development both of government, in the shape of the customs service and of trade protection, and of politics, in the form of links with mercantile interests. The cloth trade also encouraged a close interest in the politics of the Low Countries, and this industry interacted with the dynastic and political strategies that led to foreign intervention in civil war in England.

The Wars of the Roses climaxed with the replacement of the Yorkist Richard III by the Tudor Henry VII (r. 1485–1509) as a result of the killing of the former and victory of the latter at the battle of Bosworth in 1485. The Tudors had a weak dynastic claim through their Lancastrian connections, but Henry VII was helped by the unpopularity of Richard III, which ensured that much of the nobility did not support him. There were, indeed, crucial defections from his side at Bosworth.

Even so, Henry had to cope with subsequent Yorkist plots, including a full-scale rebellion in 1487 that was defeated at the battle of Stoke, the true end of the Wars of the Roses. The Yorkist army was ostensibly fighting for Edward VI, Edward, Earl of Warwick, nephew of Edward IV, who in fact was impersonated by Lambert Simnel, probably the son of an Oxford tradesman. Another nephew, John, 1st Earl of Lincoln, played a key role in the rising. He was killed in the battle and the captured Simnel was given a menial role in the royal kitchens.

This invasion/rebellion proved the last of a sequence that had started with Henry of Lancaster's against Richard II in 1399. Plots and royal anxiety, nevertheless, continued for decades thereafter, leading, under the restlessly anxious Henry VIII, to the execution of those with some possible claim on the throne. Henry VII, however, had strengthened the Tudor claim by marrying Elizabeth of York, the daughter of Edward IV. He thus joined his branch of the House of Lancaster to that of York.

The end of civil war in England and the consolidation of royal authority in Scotland under the vigorous James IV (r. 1488–1513) each provided opportunities for stronger central government. This strengthening in part took the form of new institutions, but there was also a focusing of authority and patronage on the monarch. A determined attempt was made to limit the private armed forces of nobles, and Henry VII also placed people under bonds (financial guarantees) for good behaviour. The battle of Nibley Green, fought in 1470 between Lord William Berkeley and Viscount Lisle, turned out to be the last private battle on English soil.

The focus on the monarch led to an increase in the effectiveness of royal justice, but also, in a recurrence of the pattern in earlier centuries, to a use of this justice to advance royal interests that struck many as extortionate and unfair. This situation led to a reaction when Henry VII died. Two unpopular ministers, Sir Richard Empson and Edmund Dudley, were executed, a dramatic instance of the ruthless opportunism of the new king, Henry VIII (r. 1509–47).

However, under Henry VIII, the same process of raising revenues was renewed. In large part, this was to pay for his expensive wars with France and Scotland. Indeed, the cost of these wars led to a violent popular response, in 1525, when taxes were raised in what became a far from welcome Amicable Grant, a term itself indicating that 'spin' was scarcely an invention of the late twentieth century.

Reformations

The opportunities for stronger government were to be greatly affected by the Protestant Reformation. This was part of a European movement, beginning in the German states in the late 1510s. It ended with England having a distinctive Church settlement, but the background was not exceptional. England and Scotland were parts of what sought to be a universal Church, with standard practices. There were local variations, not least attachment to particular saints and the local recruitment of clerics, but these did not detract from the wider obedience to the Papacy. Furthermore, although there were clerical abuses, popular devotion to existing religious practices was undeniable.

The Reformation led not only to change, doctrinally, liturgically and organisationally as both England and Scotland separated themselves from the universal Church. The Reformation also resulted, within England, Scotland and other states, in a religious heterodoxy as many people did not accept the changes, while others sought different changes. This heterodoxy was a challenge to royal authority and power, not least because religious toleration was treated as weakness. At the same time, the idea of transferring headship of the Church from the Papacy brought a major extension of the royal position.

In England, Parliament was used under Henry VIII to assert royal control over the Church. Henry, who had initially punished Protestants as heretics, was angered by the Pope's refusal to give him a divorce from his first wife, Katherine of Aragon, in fact an annulment declaring that no valid marriage had been contracted. By Katherine, Henry had a daughter (Mary), but not the son necessary, in his view, though not legally, to guarantee the position of the Tudor dynasty. He convinced himself that his failure to have a son was because he had married his brother's widow, a marriage permitted by Pope Julius II despite their relationship. Henry became increasingly mindful of the Biblical injunction that a man should not have sexual relations with his brother's wife. The refusal of Anne Boleyn, whom he genuinely came to love, to become Henry's mistress also played a role, as this led Henry to decide that he wanted to marry her, which pressed forward his quest for an annulment. The Pope's concern with the views of the Emperor Charles V, Katherine's nephew, ensured that negotiations for a divorce failed. This failure led to the fall of Henry's principal minister, Thomas, Cardinal Wolsey, who was dismissed as Chancellor in 1529. Significantly, there was an historical dimension. Wolsey had been charged with the offence of *praemunire*, namely breaking the statutes of 1351 and 1363 restricting papal authority in England.

In 1531, Henry became more assertive in limiting the independence of the Church. He was impressed by the argument that kings possessed imperial authority by divine gift, so that the ruler should not submit to the power of the Church. As a result, he believed papal sanction was not required for the annulment. Henry's views were taken forward with parliamentary support in 1532 as the House of Commons was antagonistic to Church officers abusing their power.

Henry finally publicly rejected Papal jurisdiction. The Act in Restraint of Appeals [to Rome] of 1533, which forbade appeals to Rome, proclaimed England as jurisdictionally self-sufficient, and was to be matched by greater pretensions on the part of James V of Scotland. Henry secretly married Anne Boleyn in 1533, and she gave birth to the future Queen Elizabeth I that year. The marriage with Katherine was annulled by the new Archbishop of Canterbury, Thomas Cranmer. This made the marriage with Anne fully valid. Princess Mary became illegitimate. In 1534, by the Act of Supremacy, Henry became the 'Supreme Head' of the English Church, and the Treason Act of 1534 made it treasonable to deny this supremacy. Conformity in belief, rather than just act, was now required. Under this Act, prominent critics such as Thomas More, the former Chancellor, and John Fisher, Bishop of Rochester, were executed in 1535.

The emphasis in England on policy and its defence led to the expression of what was, by the standards of the age, nationalism. This nationalism focused not only on present politics, lay and ecclesiastical, but also on an account of the past, while the politics, in turn, encouraged a fresh interpretation. In the preamble to the Act in Restraint of Appeals [to Rome] of 1533, it was claimed that 'by divers sundry old authentic histories and chronicles it is manifestly declared and expressed that this realm of England is an empire, and so hath been accepted in the world, governed by one supreme head and king, having the dignity and royal estate of the imperial crown of the same'. This assertion by Henry looked back to the house of Wessex's claims of overlordship in Britain in the tenth and eleventh centuries. Works on national antiquity came to the fore in the Tudor age. There was an emphasis on past glory, as with John Leland's 1544 defence of Geoffrey of Monmouth's account of King Arthur in his *Historia Regum Britanniae* (c. 1136). Anxious to accumulate information on English history, Leland, who was appointed 'King's Antiquary' in 1533, travelled extensively and wrote much, for example *De Viris Illustribus/On Famous Men*, although he published little.

Henry was no Protestant, and did not wish to see any abandonment of the Catholic faith – as was shown, after the break with Rome, by the attack on heresy with the Act of Six Articles in 1539. However, he was resolved to take charge of the Church. In 1536, injunctions specified the doctrines to be taught. Henry formulated a distinctive type of Christianity while claiming to free the English Church from the evil of papal usurpation. The rejection of miracles and relics was a major change. The impact of Henry's policies was to make the ecclesiastical situation in England dependent on English politics. Moreover, moves such as the destruction of the monasteries, nunneries and shrines hit hard at popular devotion and destroyed the sense of an unchanging religious system.

The monasteries offered rich pickings to the government, as they owned vast estates. They were dissolved (suppressed) between 1536 and 1540. The cost of wars and the pressures of patronage ensured that their land did not remain with the Crown and provide a permanent addition of revenue and therefore strength, enabling rulers to dispense with the financial support of Parliament. Instead, although some were used to endow six new bishoprics, the monastic estates were largely handed out, or sold at preferential rates, to royal supporters.

Existing landowners and royal officials were able to expand their holdings, but the process of the dissolution of the monasteries and the subsequent allocation of land led to much destruction and disruption. Monasteries were centres of religious practices such as pilgrimage, and the shrines were destroyed, not only for loot but also as a rejection of what was now presented as idolatrous. The most prominent, that of St Thomas (Becket) in Canterbury, was an historical affirmation of a set of values that Henry wished to destroy.

Monastic buildings were used for stone and lead, frequently for the houses of the new landowners. Thus, Walsingham Abbey provided the Puritan Nathaniel Bacon with stone for Stiffkey Hall. Great monasteries such as Rievaulx (Yorkshire), Bury St Edmunds and Tintern were turned into ruins. Indeed, the ruined monastery became one of the landscape markers for travellers, artists and writers from the late eighteenth century onwards. The destruction of the monasteries was a potent demonstration of Henry's will and power. The counterpoint was the palaces he built for himself, notably what was aptly called Nonsuch.

At the same time, destruction was a key element, for much of the wealth gained was spent on military preparations and war. War with France and Spain in the 1540s proved extraordinarily expensive and led to high taxation and the debasement of the coinage. Combined with inflation, these measures ensured serious economic and social strains.

As centres of local communities, monasteries and nunneries were important providers of education and other social benefits, and these functions were greatly disrupted. In part, the resulting need was met by a new philanthropy, some of it centred on the foundation of grammar schools. There was also a pressure for public provision, which helped lead to the successive pieces of legislation of 1531, 1536, 1572, 1598 and 1601 that comprised the Tudor Poor Law, although the social problems that this responded to were wider-ranging in their cause.

This Poor Law had a resonance in discussion about modern British politics in 2012. The novelist Hilary Mantel, a sympathetic chronicler of Henry's chief minister of the 1530s, Thomas Cromwell, argued that his 1536 legislation was more enlightened in its attitudes than the then Conservative-led coalition government. She claimed that the latter was 'going back to the Middle Ages', in other words the situation before Cromwell. This was a poorly thought-through comparison.

Concern about the Dissolution of the Monasteries ensured that Henry faced a serious challenge in 1536. Opposition to his policies, particularly towards the Church, as well as anxiety about rumours of new taxes, triggered a major rebellion in the North of England, the Pilgrimage of Grace. The reaction indicated the extent of popular concern about political and religious developments, and the role of religion in helping to rally support. The army of the Pilgrims was to rally round the sacred banner of St Cuthbert which was brought by the Durham contingent. The Pilgrims contrasted 'the whole body of the realm' with 'evil-disposed persons' in the King's council: a contrast with a lengthy medieval pedigree but one made more complex by the religious dimension.

Using true faith as an element of judgment when considering claims about tyranny offered a seriously subversive means for dissent across the religious spectrum. As with later episodes, such as the civil wars that broke out in 1638–42, a general cause for opposition was combined with specific political agendas, so that, in 1536, there were complaints about the Treason Act, the Succession Act of 1536 (which enabled the monarch to name his successor – a measure that would deal with the argument that Henry's divorce from Katherine was illegitimate), and unpopular governmental practices.

As with the Peasants' Revolt in 1381, tension was assuaged by royal concessions, but there was subsequent repression as Henry, who never intended to fulfil these concessions, was released from his promises by further revolts. This ensured that there was no Parliament at York to settle grievances. Furthermore, the Pilgrimage of Grace did not stop the dissolution of the monasteries, nor the concurrent attack on saint worship. Instead, there was a brutal treatment of the former rebels while the opportunity was taken to execute most of the survivors of the blood royal outside Henry's immediate family. This was as part of a more widespread violent treatment of those whom Henry distrusted, one in which the law was readily manipulated by a suspicious and insecure king ready to use deceit to overcome the reality of problems.

At the same time, Henry's suspicions were manipulated, as in 1536 when the conservatives at court, joined in this case by Thomas Cromwell, Henry's key minister, (falsely) alleged that Anne was being unfaithful, in order to overthrow her. Anne was executed, and Elizabeth became a bastard. Cromwell himself was to be executed in 1540 when the conservative faction exploited his unwillingness to support Henry's favour for Katherine Howard, whom the king married on the day of the execution. In turn, her alleged adultery led to her execution in 1542. Katherine certainly recklessly showed favour to young courtiers.

More than executions were involved in Henry's politics and suspicions. Uneasiness about the security situation far from London led the government in 1536–43 to push through Union with Wales so that it was all assimilated into the English governmental, parliamentary and legal systems.

Religious change under Henry helped ensure that there was a shift of psychological possibilities as far as the people were concerned: the ending of Purgatory and the concomitant practice of offering prayers for the dead destroyed the links between the communities of the living and the dead. In contrast, the production of an official English Bible in 1537, followed by the instruction to every parish church to purchase a copy, was a marked extension of the authority of print that expanded the possibilities for readers and listeners of reaching their own conclusions, and also encouraged literacy. The possibilities of state direction of the

Church were linked to those of the new technology of printing. The authoritative nature of the Bible was taken further with the King James Version of 1611. Printing was also to reduce the impact of regional linguistic differences.

Religious change was pushed further under Henry's only son, Edward VI (r. 1547–53), the child of his third marriage: to Jane Seymour. Edward and his ministers very much took England in the direction of Protestantism, leading to a violent, but unsuccessful, Catholic rebellion in the West Country in 1549, the Prayer Book Rebellion. Edward came to the throne aged nine, and his reign was dominated by a feuding aristocratic Council. Initially, the major figure was Edward's uncle, Edward, Duke of Somerset, who became Protector of the Realm when Henry died. He supported Protestantism and also a degree of governmental responsiveness to social problems. In particular, the enclosure of common land by landlords led to much criticism, with which Somerset sympathised. However, when opposition to enclosure and to high rents led in 1549 to Kett's Rebellion in East Anglia, this apparent threat to the social order helped discredit Somerset.

He was replaced in 1549 by John Dudley, Earl of Warwick, a successful soldier, who in 1551 was made Duke of Northumberland. Northumberland, who had his rival Somerset executed, pushed England in a more radically Protestant direction, not least with the 1552 Prayer Book. Furthermore, churches were transformed. Their interiors were whitewashed and stripped of imagery, such as statues and wallpaintings. Their removal helped shatter the pious rituals that gave many people a sense of value.

This new order, however, was threatened by Edward's poor health, culminating in his death in July 1553. Faced with the prospect that a firm Catholic, in the person of Mary, Henry's daughter by his first marriage (to Katherine of Aragon), would succeed, Northumberland backed the succession of Lady Jane Grey, who had a weak claim (as a granddaughter of Henry VII through his second daughter) but offered the prospect of continued Protestantism and of government by the Duke, who married Lady Jane to his son. However, when Edward died, support rallied to Mary rather than the unpopular Northumberland. Acting in a decisive manner, and drawing on a degree of popular support, Mary gained the throne. Northumberland and Lady Jane were beheaded.

The Catholic reaction under Mary (r. 1553–8) was to be cut short by her childless death, ensuring that Mary was chiefly remembered as a persecutor, with nearly 300 Protestants burnt at the stake during her reign, including prominent figures such as Thomas Cranmer, Archbishop of Canterbury. London, Kent and Sussex had a disproportionately high number of Protestant martyrs, being geographically nearest to Continental Protestantism, and also most exposed to royal power and attention.

One refugee, John Foxe, published in 1563 his *Acts and Monuments of Matters Most Special and Memorable Happening in the Church*, popularly known as the *Book of Martyrs*. This oft-reprinted account of religious history included a martyrology that was extremely influential in propagating an image of Catholic cruelty and Protestant bravery that was to sustain a strong anti-Catholic tradition for over 250 years. Foxe presented an account of England as a kingdom that had been in the forefront of the advance towards the Christian faith, and that had not had to be converted by missionaries from Rome. This claim for a separate religious identity encouraged the sense of the English as a chosen people. Such an account might seem a negative, exclusionist definition of nationhood, but the real, as well as apparent, hostile character of international Catholicism helped justify this position. After an order of 1571, cathedral churches acquired copies of the *Book of Martyrs*, and many parish churches chose to do likewise.

Alongside the religious theme, there was also a significant geopolitical one in Mary's reign. Her important Spanish heritage, as the daughter of Katherine of Aragon, helped lead to marriage to her Habsburg relative, Philip II of Spain. This marriage was part of the Habsburg plan to dominate Western Europe and counter French expansionism. The resulting war with France, however, saw the English crown in 1558 lose Calais, the last of the gains from the Hundred Years' War.

The Protestant settlement under Mary's half-sister Elizabeth I (r. 1558–1603), the daughter of Henry's second marriage, to Anne Boleyn, was moderate by the standards of Edward VI's reign. Elizabeth maintained the authority of bishops. Her choice to be termed Supreme Governor of the Church of England, more modest than Supreme Head, may have reflected her position as a woman, but was to be continued by all her successors.

Elizabeth's religious settlement was unsuccessfully resisted by the Catholic Northern Rising of 1569. The rebellion itself indicated widespread popular support for Catholicism in the north of England. Elizabeth herself was excommunicated and formally deposed by the Pope in 1570. The Catholic challenge focused on Elizabeth's cousin, Mary, Queen of Scots. Through the marriage of her grandfather James IV to Henry VII's daughter Margaret in 1503, she had a good claim to the succession, if Elizabeth remained unmarried.

In Scotland, Mary, Queen of Scots, attempted to reverse the Protestant changes pushed through by the Scottish Parliament in 1560 – changes that ensured that on her formal entry into Edinburgh in 1561 she was confronted by Protestant symbols. In a revival of earlier Crown-noble confrontation, albeit in a new context, Mary was thwarted by the baronial Lords of the Congregation. They forced her to abdicate in 1567, in favour of her infant son, James VI. In 1568, she fled to England where she was imprisoned. Her connivance in plots against Elizabeth led to her being beheaded in 1587.

Mary's overthrow in 1567 ended the danger that Protestant England would have a Catholic northern neighbour. Instead, despite important differences, there was a measure of Protestant fellow-feeling and co-operation between England and Scotland, and this was to look towards more significant episodes of alliance in the seventeenth century. It also contrasted markedly with the longstanding English attempts to dominate Scotland that had been given fresh drive in the 1540s, only to fail as a result of the military problems, the intractabilities of Scottish politics, and contrary French intervention.

Under Elizabeth, there was a deliberate shift in strategy, to ensuring that a friendly (i.e. Protestant) government was in power in Edinburgh, rather than trying to rule the country directly. To this end, the English four times under Elizabeth sent expeditions into Scotland, but these never attempted to go beyond the Firth of Forth. The overthrow of the French regency by the Lords of Congregation in 1560 would have been impossible without the involvement of an English army and, even more significantly, navy. Furthermore, at times of disquiet, large forces were mustered in northern England, which may have helped to ensure a favourable outcome in Scotland.

Elizabeth's England

A more clear-cut challenge to England was presented in 1588 by the Armada, a Spanish attempt to send a major fleet up the English Channel in order to cover an invasion of England from the Spanish Netherlands (modern Belgium). The English fleet, smaller but with superior sailing qualities, inflicted damage as the Spaniards sailed along in the Channel, before a night attack using fireships disrupted the Armada off Calais, causing further losses in the subsequent battle. Preparations for an invasion were abandoned. Sailing home around the British Isles, the Armada lost many ships as a result of storms.

This victory came to play a major role in English identity. Providence was seen in a victory that owed much to the problems of the Spanish navy, luck and favourable winds, as well as to the heroism and fighting quality of the English navy. This luck fuelled the development of belief in a Providential sanction to English Protestantism, a Sanction which was confirmed in 1688 by the 'Protestant Wind' that helped William of Orange, later William III, overthrow James II. What to us illustrates the tenuous survival of Elizabeth's regime, to contemporaries displayed the unassailable nature of divine approval.

Despite serious problems both domestic and international, Elizabeth maintained control throughout her long reign. In England, there was no comparison to the civil conflict in France (the French Wars of Religion), Ireland or, more briefly, Scotland. Instead, the Elizabethan order was entrenched through longevity. This was particularly the case with the religious settlement, not least because the number who had experienced a different situation as adults gradually died out. An increasing percentage of the population had been educated in a Protestant Christianity, and fewer had lived in an unchallenged world of Catholicism. Elizabeth was the first ruler not to look into men's consciences. Their outward conformity was all she sought. Furthermore, the new religious settlement was associated with an English patriotism and, indeed, it helped define it; the same process occurring in Scotland. In modern secular Britain, the impact of the reiterated combination of a particular formulation of Crown and Church is difficult to grasp, but it was successful in ensuring that the Reformation took deep roots.

Begun in 1585, in large part in order to thwart Spain's supression of the (Protestant) Dutch Revolt, war with Spain continued until 1604. Although Spanish intervention in support of rebellion against English control in Ireland failed, as did the rebellion, however victory against Spain proved elusive. Moreover, the financial burden of war produced serious political difficulties that came to a head in parliamentary opposition in the 1590s. Such opposition was significant. Henry VIII's use of Parliament to legitimate his dynastic and constitutional objectives had increased its frequency and role. Despite Henry's wishes, and largely due to the minority of Edward VI, parliamentary management had become a more important issue. With the Crown in Parliament as the source of sovereign authority, parliamentary legislation became more common.

There were other related dimensions to the political difficulties of the 1590s, particularly religion and the succession. Within the established Church, Puritanism, a tendency within the established Church, pressed for more radical Church reform leading to a more severe, Calvinistic organisation and theology. Expressions of discontent focused on the role of bishops and the nature of clerical vestments. At the same time, the political and religious system and the anticipated Protestant succession were anathema to Catholics, some of whom had plotted the assassination of the Queen. Her role was seen as crucial, and this also explains why Robert, 2nd Earl of Essex, a failed royal favourite, planned to seize her in order to secure his position. This unsuccessful conspiracy led to his execution in 1601.

Such instability was a background to the plays of the period. This was a period not only of the rise of a more intense level of public politics, part of it responding to Court and parliamentary events, but also of a more public culture. The popular enjoyment of drama was one of the highpoints of the age. In Scotland, theatre developed, with works by Sir David Lindsay and others, but it was essentially in a Court setting. In England, in contrast, public patronage and the exigencies and opportunities of the commercial marketplace were important. The Theatre, the first purpose-built public playhouse in England, was opened in London in 1576, the Curtain in 1577, and the Globe Theatre in 1599. The Reformation had weakened patterns of control over expression, providing new opportunities for the theatre. William Shakespeare's plays expressed the aspirations and tensions of the emerging nation state, while their vocabulary and phrases came to occupy a major position in the language.

British society

What was the nature of this society? It is all too easy, watching modern television and film adaptations, to assume that it was similar to ours. This was far from the case, not least in the basic details of life experience and demographic expectation. After marked growth in 1500–1650, in England from under 2.5 million to about five million, and in Scotland to about one million, the population ceased to rise at the same rate. In England, it fell between 1660 and 1690, probably due to enteric fevers and gastric diseases, and in Scotland it declined in the 1690s. In many areas, the death-rate crises of 1696–9, 1727–30 and 1741–2 wiped out the growth of the intervening years. Despite these crises, life expectancy at birth showed an important upwards trend, from an average lifespan of about 30 for those born in the 1680s to 42 by the 1750s. There was no official census until 1801, but the population of England and Wales probably rose from 5.07 million in 1666 to 6.20 million in 1751. Thereafter, as the demographic regime changed, the population of England and Wales rose rapidly, to reach 8.66 million in 1801.

England dominated the British Isles demographically, although less so than today. In 1689, the English population was about 4.9 million compared to about 2.0 million for Ireland, about 1.2 million for Scotland, and about 0.3 million for Wales. Although the bulk of the population lived in villages, hamlets and farmsteads, a growing percentage lived in towns and cities.

The major role of agriculture ensured that much of the population lived in the most fertile areas, such as southern and eastern England, the fertile lowlands of South Wales (for example, the Vale of Glamorgan) and the central lowlands of Scotland. Nevertheless, the leading role of agriculture also meant that a greater percentage than today lived in areas that were less attractive for farming, but where a living could still be earned from the soil. This was true, for example, of upland pasture areas. In the countryside, parishes that attracted immigration tended to be those that offered opportunities for cottage industry. The availability of common land could be very important here, not least in providing scope for the increased population. Yet, throughout Britain at the local level, there were major variations, reflecting the extent to which a national demographic regime was both superimposed on, and mediated through, local patterns of activity.

The relationship between population and household structure was very different from that in modern Britain. Barring occasional bigamies, wife sales and aristocratic Bills of Divorce, marriage was irreversible. As a consequence, it ended only with the death of one of the partners, or with a desertion that involved flight from the community. Marriage was also central to sex, procreation and the upbringing of children, a matrix that has been greatly changed in modern Britain. Most childbearing was within marriage. Despite the absence of effective contraceptives and of safe, let alone legal, abortion, recorded illegitimacy rates were low.

In contrast to modern Britain, many people never lived in a sexual relationship, although some of those who did not do so would have relied on casual sex, which overwhelmingly meant prostitution. Many men and women never married, and marriages were generally late. At the end of the seventeenth century, English men married on average at about 28 and women at about 27. Childbearing was thus postponed until an average of more than ten years past puberty, which itself occurred later than in modern Britain.

Law and social convention gave authority to fathers and husbands. However, in practice, their authority was often tempered by the dynamics of family life, the play of personality, and the need for co-operation if families were to cope with challenges. Social politics were also hierarchical. They could be the subject of humorous overturning as in Francis Beaumont's play *The Knight of the Burning Pestle* (1607), in which an apprentice, Jasper, marries Luce, the daughter of his master, a merchant, against the latter's will, as he favours another suitor. Luce is seized by her parents and locked up. Feigning death, Jasper is taken into the house in a coffin where he frightens the merchant by appearing as a ghost, and thus gains his consent. Thomas Dekker's comedy *The Shoemaker's Holiday* (1599) has a nobleman disguise himself as a shoemaker to pursue his love for another shoemaker's daughter.

Reality was generally far bleaker. The plight of young love, at the mercy of the power of parents or guardians, was a frequent theme in drama, as in Thomas Middleton and Thomas Dekker's *The Roaring Girl* (1610). Status and authority were both involved. In Philip Massinger's play *A New Way to Pay Old Debts* (c. 1622), the greed of the villain, Sir Giles Overreach, is focused on the calculation of social advantage through family marriages, and failure leads to his becoming mad.

For all, defences against disease remained flimsy, not least because of the limited nature of medical knowledge. There was no comparison to modern suppositions that there should be a medical cure for everything. Instead, folk cures and prayer were the remedies open to most people. Modern attitudes towards holistic approaches to medicine and modern knowledge of placebo effects, suggest that these remedies would have been far from worthless. Indeed they might have been more potent than today given contemporary belief in their appropriateness, if not efficacy.

There were advances in a range of treatments, especially in the prevention of smallpox, one of the most serious diseases. Among those it claimed was Queen Mary in 1694. After 1665, when the Great Plague hit, killing nearly 100,000 people in London alone, smallpox replaced bubonic plague as the most feared disease. As smallpox was airborne, growing urbanisation and a rise in population increased vulnerability to the disease, and therefore the ubiquity of scarring on survivors of smallpox. In major urban areas, the disease became endemic as well as epidemic, and this proved particularly deadly to infants and children.

Smallpox, like much else, was also socially selective. The poor lived at a higher population density than the wealthy. In addition, smallpox viruses remained viable for up to a year and could be contracted via clothing or bedding. The poor were less able to afford to destroy clothing and bedding after a death, and so were more vulnerable.

Initially, inoculation was of limited value as a bar to a serious attack of smallpox, although it became safer after the Suttonian method of inserting only the smallest possible amount of infectious matter was widely adopted, from about 1768. Vaccination, a safer method, was not performed until 1796, but inoculation lessened the potential breeding ground for smallpox.

No comparable progress was made in fighting other serious problems. These included diseases that would not now be fatal to healthy Westerners with access to good medical care, such as intestinal diseases. In the eighteenth and nineteenth century, typhus, typhoid, influenza, cholera, dysentery, chicken-pox, measles, scarlet fever and syphilis were all serious problems. Mobility and international trade increased the ease with which epidemics could spread, although, with some diseases, exposure also brought a measure of resistance. Other conditions, that can now be cured or held at bay, were debilitating. Malnutrition stunted growth, hit energy levels and reduced resistance to ill-health, notably in the 1590s. Poor diet encouraged colon parasitic infection, hepatitis and salmonella. Alcohol and opium were the only painkillers, and cheap laudanum was a universal panacea and the basis of standard medicines.

There was no system of health provision. Skilled practitioners were few, generally concentrated in towns, and expensive. Medical treatments, such as blistering or mercury, could be inappropriate, and were often painful, dangerous or enervating. Surgery was primitive and performed without anaesthetics.

Moreover, there were serious environmental problems. Many industrial processes were dangerous to others besides the workers. Dressing and tanning leather polluted water supplies, while the kilns of brick and tile works produced smoke and fumes. There were restrictions on individual noxious practices, for example the pollution of water supplies by some industrial processes, but there was no systematic scrutiny or drive for improvements. Urine was widely used for washing cloth well into the eighteenth century.

Living conditions were also a major problem. Crowded housing conditions, particularly the sharing of beds, helped spread diseases, especially respiratory infections. Most dwellings were neither warm nor dry, and it was very difficult to get clothes dry. This discouraged the washing of clothes, and also led to the wearing of layers of clothes, many of them thick, so that exposure to the wet should not lead to wet skin. The prevalence of work out of doors and of transport on foot or horseback greatly increased exposure to adverse weather. By modern standards, breath, teeth and skin must have been repellent, and houses would have been very smelly.

People were vulnerable to fire, most obviously with the Great Fire of London which raged for four days in 1666. Wood and thatch burned readily, and fire-fighting faced many limitations.

In Devon, Tiverton was hit hard in 1726, 1730 and, especially, 1731, the last leading to an Act of Parliament that all roofs thereafter should be of lead, slate or tile; while, of other Devon towns, Crediton lost 460 houses to a savage fire in 1743, and much of Honiton was rebuilt after fires in 1747 and 1765.

Humans were also very much at war with the animal world. Animals capable of inflicting death – bears and wolves – had long been wiped out. However, foxes attacked farm animals, rabies was a problem among the dog population, rats were a serious issue, and bed bugs, lice, fleas and tapeworms were real and widespread horrors.

It is difficult to recreate an impression of the smell and dirt of the period. Ventilation was limited, while drains blocked. Humans lived close to animals and dunghills, and this damaged health. Manure stored near buildings was hazardous and could contaminate the water supply. Effluent from undrained privies and animals' pens flowed across streets and also into houses through generally porous walls. Privies with open soil pits lay directly alongside dwellings and under bedrooms; although, alongside the particularly parlous state of the poor, disease was also a social leveller. The 5th Earl of Plymouth (1751–99), who was described as 'a fine fat round English Lord, loves to eat', was, by 1794, 'in a very bad way, for he is very near blind, and his legs are so swelled that it is thought he is going into a dropsy'. His son and heir had an even shorter life (1789–1833). Poor nutrition lowered resistance to disease and to the psychological impact of adversity. Fruit and vegetables were both seasonal and expensive.

As far as the poor were concerned, there was scant understanding of the problems posed by unemployment and under-employment, and such hardships were treated as self-inflicted and thus deserving of neglect or punishment. The standard precept of care was that it should discriminate between the deserving and the undeserving. This religio-moral principle was applied on grounds of age, health and gender, and not with reference to employment or income. Thus, the infirm, the elderly, the young and women with children were the prime beneficiaries of poor relief, while the able-bodied, whether in low-paid employment or unemployed, were denied it.

At the same time, government action in many aspects sought to benefit all. For example, there was intervention in the grain market, which, in England, was regularised with the issue of Books of Orders from 1586. In response to the threat of grain shortages – a serious challenge to public order – Justices of the Peace were obliged to determine the availability of surplus grain and to ensure that it was brought to market. Focusing on distribution and allocation as cause and solution ensured a need for information.

James VI and I

Tensions over the role of Parliament caused major problems during the reign of James I of England (r. 1603–25), who was also James VI of Scotland (r. 1567–1625). The Catholic Gunpowder Plot aimed against James in 1605 was a testimony to this role, as the planned explosion was linked to a meeting of Parliament in Westminster.

The anniversary celebration of the failure of the conspiracy was to add a new date to the marking of the year in a Protestant fashion, which was a replacement to the earlier dominance of the year by the commemoration of saints' days. This process had already been taken forward under Elizabeth, not least as the war with Spain (1585–1604) fostered national consciousness, providing a new focus for the commemoration of national history. This history was expounded in a number of works, most notably in Raphael Holinshed's *Chronicles* (1577). Printed maps, such as those by John Speed, provided another image of the country, one fixed through printing.

Moreover, war with Spain encouraged a different placing of Britain, one in which a global, notably trans-Atlantic, role appeared necessary and inevitable. As popular allegiance to Protestantism grew, so new national days of celebration recalling recent Protestant history became popular. Church bells were rung every 17 November to celebrate the accession of Elizabeth in 1558 and thus the end of Catholic rule. The defeat of the Armada provided another anniversary.

Although a Protestant, James I, however, proved a figure whom it was difficult to incorporate into heroic accounts. Already, as James VI of Scotland, a monarch who had had to cope with the shifts and expedients of a weak position, James I was the beneficiary of Tudor–Stuart dynastic links. He came to the throne as a result of the marriage of Henry VII's daughter Margaret with James IV, combined with the failure of Henry VIII's three legitimate children to have children of their own. James went south to claim his new crown in 1603, a transition managed with far less difficulty than had been anticipated, and stayed in England, except for one visit. He was therefore less exposed than his Scottish predecessors to the impact of quarrels between Scottish lords, or to their defiance of royal authority.

Scotland, however, remained an independent state, governed by the Scottish Privy Council. Despite James's hopes for a 'union of love', or at least a measure of administrative and economic union between England and Scotland, the union remained essentially personal. There was fear in England about the legal and constitutional implications, and the Westminster Parliament rejected a parliamentary or legal bond.

As ruler both in Scotland and in England, James lacked charisma and found it difficult to win respect or affection. His policies were mistrusted and he could not avoid mounting debts. However, he acquired a degree of competence in the difficult management of English parliamentary and religious politics, as he had done with Scottish factionalism. In England and Scotland, there was no breakdown of control or stability akin to those in France and the Holy Roman Empire (Germany) in the 1610s and early 1620s. Moreover, control was extended in Ireland where English law and custom was imposed and much of Ulster was confiscated. Large portions of it were settled by Scots.

The union of the Crowns in 1603 helped lead to the demilitarisation of the Borders of England and Scotland, which had been a region that was particularly difficult to control. This was an aspect of a more general shift towards a monopolisation of force by public authorities, one that left a testimony in the shape of the increasingly dilapidated state of castles, notably in England.

Nevertheless, many aristocrats under both Elizabeth and James retained a military capability. Great landowners maintained arsenals, not only of muskets, pikes and halberds but even of artillery: Elizabeth's favourite, Robert, 1st Earl of Leicester (c. 1532–88), son of the Northumberland executed in 1553, and grandson of the Dudley executed in 1510, had a large number of cannon at his seat at Kenilworth Castle. Even a minor noble like Lord Norreys had some cannon at his seat in Berkshire. A coterie of armed followers remained an essential part of aristocratic status for many aristocrats, and recruiting by affinity continued to be a major way of raising troops into the early seventeenth century. However, under James, there was a serious running-down of military capacity, which had deleterious consequences when war broke out with Spain and France in the 1620s, and which also helped handicap Charles I when he faced rebellion in Scotland.

Charles I and the Civil War

The personal union between Scotland and England, which James termed Great Britain, broke down as a result of the policies of Charles I (r. 1625–49). Lacking common sense, flexibility and pragmatism, Charles was devious and untrustworthy. His belief in order and in the dignity of kingship led Charles to take an unsympathetic and arrogant attitude to disagreement. Tension over his extraordinary financial demands, notably Ship Money, and over apparently crypto-Catholic ecclesiastical policies, sapped support for Charles in England, but the breakdown occurred in Scotland. There, Charles's commitment to religious change, particularly a stronger episcopacy and a new liturgy, and his aggressive treatment of critical Scottish views, led to the Bishops' Wars (1639–40). This was the start of the Civil Wars, and it was symptomatic of the whole period of conflict: Charles mishandled the situation and lost, religion played a major role in the war, and it involved different parts of the British Isles, each of which were themselves divided.

The crisis led Charles to turn to Parliament in England, but the period of his 'Personal Rule' without Parliament since 1629 had generated a series of grievances and much fear about his intentions. In an angry and desperate attempt to rebuild the political system, Parliament turned on Charles's ministers and policies. Charles abandoned Thomas, 1st Earl of Strafford, his most unpopular minister, who was tried and executed in 1641, and he conceded some points, including the abolition of prerogative courts. However, Charles responded firmly to attacks on Church government.

In an atmosphere of mounting crisis, the need to raise an army to deal with a major Catholic rising in Ireland in November 1641 polarised the situation. Debate over who was to control this army exacerbated tensions over parliamentary pressure for a change in Church government. The power and authority of both Crown and Parliament came to the fore and in conspicuous opposition to each other. Charles resorted to violence, invading Parliament on 4 January 1642, in order to seize the 'Five Members', his leading opponents, but they had already fled by river to the City of London, a centre of hostility to Charles.

Both sides then prepared for war, with the south and east of England, the navy and many of the large towns backing Parliament, while Charles, who left London on 10 January 1642, enjoyed greatest support in Wales, and rural parts of north and west England. Each side had support in every region and social group, and the relationship between religious and political differences, and economic groups, was complex, but parliamentary support was strongest in the most economically-advanced regions. Belief, especially religious allegiance, was crucial in explaining variations in support. Charles was the focus for powerful feelings of honour, loyalty and duty, while many parliamentary supporters were vehement in their hostility to the Catholicism in Charles's circle and to the crypto-Catholic tendencies in the established Church ascribed to William Laud, Archbishop of Canterbury. The policies of the latter led to a violent reaction that included the destruction of Church fittings such as altar rails that were seen as Catholic.

Fighting in England started in July 1642. Having narrowly defeated the main Parliamentary army at Edgehill on 23 October, Charles failed, in difficult circumstances, at Turnham Green on 13 November, to press home his advance on London. In 1643, the Royalists overran most of western England, capturing Bristol; but, in 1644, an army fielded by the Presbyterians who dominated Scotland entered northern England on the side of Parliament. At Marston Moor near York on 2 July 1644, a Scots/Parliamentary army defeated the Royalists. Oliver Cromwell, originally a member of the Huntingdonshire gentry, commanded the Parliamentary cavalry. Northern England was then lost to the Royalists.

Moreover, at Naseby on 14 June 1645 the New Model Army, the major Parliamentary force, with Cromwell again in command of the cavalry, destroyed the leading Royalist field army. Three months later, the Royalist army in Scotland under James, 1st Marquis of Montrose, was defeated. Defeats in battle led to the fall of the remaining Royalist positions. On 5 May 1646, Charles gave himself up.

Parliamentary victory was due in part to the support of the wealthiest regions of England and Scotland, and to the folly of Charles; but fighting ability, command skills and chance also played major roles. The Parliamentarians were fortunate to be able to win before war-weariness sapped their war effort. Having won, the victors fell out. Parliament, the army leadership and the Scots clashed over Church government, negotiations with Charles, control of the army and its substantial arrears in pay.

Cromwell and the Interregnum

Civil war resumed in 1648 when the Scots invaded England on behalf of Charles, who, in return, had agreed to recognise Presbyterianism. There was also a series of Royalist risings, notably in Kent and South Wales. All, however, were crushed, with the invading Scots defeated at Preston.

The army, under Oliver Cromwell, followed up its victory, by purging Parliament in order to stop it negotiating with the King (Pride's Purge). Charles was then tried and, on 30 January 1649, executed for treason against the people. England was declared a republic for the only time in its history. Royal coats of arms and other devices were removed and statues destroyed. Charles's sons, Charles, who claimed the throne as Charles II, and his brother James, Duke of York, later James II and VII, lived abroad as exiles. The republican revolution encouraged speculation about new purposes and methods for government, as well as actual innovations in government.

Cromwell pressed on to conquer first Ireland and then Scotland. The execution of Charles I in 1649 entrenched the radicalism of the new regime, just as the failure to demobilise after war ended in 1646 had entrenched the role of military concerns.

Yet, this was an authoritarian radicalism that did not go as far toward religious or political freedom as others wished to go. Thus, the Levellers' movement, which came to the fore in 1647, was suppressed by Cromwell. They had pressed for universal male suffrage, but Cromwell was not interested in democracy.

The Levellers were succeeded by the True Levellers, or Diggers, who, seeing private property as the consequence of the Fall (the exclusion of Adam and Eve from the Garden of Eden), pressed the people's rights to common property. The Diggers tried to dig the common on St George's Hill, Surrey in 1649, but were dispersed by the army and angry locals, suffering the same fate subsequently at Cobham. The Diggers' leader, Gerrard Winstanley, indicated the mobility of British society. Born in Wigan, he was apprenticed in London, but his failure in trade led to his becoming a Surrey cowhand.

Cromwell's decisive victories over Scottish armies at Dunbar (1650) and Worcester (1651) were followed by the fall of Scotland, the first time it had been conquered. Scotland could no longer serve as an alternative political model to England. The Scottish Parliament and executive council were abolished, the power of the Scottish nobility was curtailed and measures were taken to adopt English law. In 1654, Scotland, alongside England, Ireland and Wales, was represented in the Parliament nominated by Cromwell and his council of officers.

Cromwell had seized power in 1653, when he closed the Rump Parliament (comprising what was left after the purge of December 1648). He became Lord Protector, and, in 1657, hereditary Protector, with a ceremony that included much of the ceremonial of English monarchy. Cromwell's, however, was a military regime, shot through with an intolerant sense of divine purpose: the emphasis was on godliness rather than toleration. He found it difficult to find a Parliament that satisfied him.

In 1655, largely in response to Royalist risings (which indicated considerable support for the Royalist claimant, Charles II), authority in the localities was entrusted to major-generals, instructed to preserve security and to create a Puritan, godly and efficient state. These were unpopular goals. Hostility to an oppressive Puritanism that, for the sake of continued reformation and godliness, repressed popular rituals deemed superstitious or profane, such as Christmas and dancing around the maypole, fused with resentment of the illegal, radical and repressive regime. The granting, in 1656, of permission for Jews to settle in England was not popular. The use of major-generals as agents of local control helped to undermine the fragile legitimacy of the government, which anyway suffered greatly from its origins in republican regicide.

Cromwell died in 1658, but his successor as Protector, his ineffective son Richard, unable to command authority and lacking the support of the army, lost power the following May. The resulting political crisis, which saw the bitterly divided army opposed to the reconvened Rump Parliament, did not, however, have an inevitable outcome. The republic was weak and unstable, but it was not certain that Charles II would come to power. Indeed, George Booth's rebellion against the Rump was defeated in August 1659. There was support for a republican future, but this support was divided. The crisis was finally resolved with the Restoration: the army commander in Scotland, George Monck, marched south, occupied London, and restored order and a moderate Parliament that, in turn, recalled Charles II (r. 1660–85).

The Restoration monarchy, 1660–88

The new King possessed the skills his father so patently lacked. Approachable and charming, Charles was also flexible and pragmatic. The Restoration was popular. However, this popularity did not solve political problems, and was not to last. Charles II neither set out to rule without Parliament, as his father had done, nor to restore the prerogative taxation and jurisdictional institutions of the 1630s, such as Ship Money and Star Chamber. However, the subsequent legislation passed by Parliament from 1641 was repealed, as was the *ad hoc* union with Scotland introduced under Cromwell. In addition, the 1662 religious settlement re-imposed an Anglican order in England and Wales which left Protestant Nonconformists alienated.

The new political order was to unravel, in part due to Charles's policies but more generally due to the extent to which the Civil War and the Interregnum had created a new political and religious world. In this, pluralism and the expression of opinions were to the fore, and there were expectations that the decisions of government would be debated and contradicted.

In the meanwhile, human vulnerability was underlined by the Great Plague of 1665 and the Great Fire of London the following year. Concern about Charles's religious intentions, and anxiety about the succession to the heirless (his only children were illegitimate) king, whose brother, James, was a Catholic, snowballed in 1678 into a crisis. In turn, the concerns about Catholic influences that spawned the alleged Popish Plot of that year led into the Exclusion Crisis (1678–81): an attempt to use Parliament to exclude James from the succession. Its supporters were known as Whigs, and those opposed to Exclusion as Tories.

Exclusion failed. Unlike in 1638–42, the Crown retained control of Scotland and Ireland, while, within England, there was a reluctance to risk civil war anew. Whig failure was followed, in 1681–5, by a Tory reaction which included the persecution of Whig leaders and the abrogation of the charter of the City of London in 1683.

James II (and VII of Scotland) came to the throne in 1685, but one of Charles's illegitimate sons, the Protestant James, Duke of Monmouth, invaded. He was defeated at Sedgemoor and subsequently executed. Similarly, a rebellion, by Archibald, 9th Duke of Argyll, in Scotland against James failed.

James was encouraged, both by these successes and by the difficulties he encountered with his first Parliament, to press on and follow his inclinations. These were in favour of a more autocratic politics that was intended to support Catholicising policies. Appointing Catholics as Lord Lieutenants of counties, however, proved of limited value to James as the new men lacked the stature and connections of traditional aristocratic holders of the office. James's policies alienated the support Charles II had mustered in the early 1680s, and was particularly unwelcome to the Tories, who backed the position of the Church of England. The Whigs, already alienated, were developing notions of liberty and consent that directly challenged the practice of royal government.

James called no Parliament in 1686 and 1687, and tensions increased. They became acute in 1688 when his Catholic second wife, Mary of Modena, had a son, who therefore took precedence in the succession over Mary and Anne, his Protestant daughters by his first wife. This encouraged an upsurge in opposition in Britain, and that upsurge favoured the plans of James's nephew and son-in-law, William III of Orange, Mary's husband. The chief figure in the Protestant United Provinces (modern Netherlands), William, was the leader of opposition in Protestant Europe to the expansionism of Louis XIV of France. Louis had alarmed Protestants throughout Europe in 1685 by revoking the privileges under which French Protestants had been allowed to maintain their faith.

The Glorious Revolution

In November 1688, William invaded England, landing in Brixham after the English fleet had made only a weak effort to block him. William brought a large army and siege train with him (and also several thousand muskets to arm expected Protestant sympathisers), clearly expecting to have to mount a campaign against James's large army.

What became known as the Glorious Revolution was the last successful invasion of England, as well as a coup in which the monarch was replaced, and the political and constitutional changes that stemmed from both. Civil war appeared imminent, but James's resolve failed and he abandoned his troops. As William advanced on London and the morale of the royal army disintegrated, a vacuum of power developed. Most people did not want any breach in the hereditary succession, and William had initially claimed that he had no designs on the Crown. However, as the situation developed favourably, especially when James had been driven into exile, William made it clear that he sought the throne and would not accept it being offered to his wife.

The crisis was resolved in 1689 by stating that the throne was vacant as James had abdicated by leaving the kingdom. In fact, he had been driven out. As James's successor, William and Mary were declared joint monarchs, with the reversion to Anne only when both had died. By claiming that it was only a vacancy that was being filled, rather than an elective monarchy that was being created, it was possible to minimise the element of innovation. All Catholics were debarred from the succession.

The Glorious Revolution also launched Jacobitism, as the cause of the exiled Stuarts came to be known from the Latin for James, Jacobus. The cost of William's invasion, however, was not only a civil war that brought much suffering to Scotland and Ireland, but also a difficult war with France which lasted until 1697. Louis XIV gave James II shelter and support and sent an army to Ireland in a major attempt to maintain James in power. However, despite initial success in both Scotland and Ireland, the Jacobites were dispersed in Scotland in 1689 and defeated in Ireland, notably at the battles of the Boyne (1690) and Aughrim (1691). From 1692, William's forces were in control of Ireland. As well as shaping the political, constitutional and fiscal nature of the Revolution Settlement, the war created considerable stresses within Britain.

For eighteenth-century Whig commentators, the Glorious Revolution had totemic significance as a crucial source of difference between Britain and Continental Europe. They saw religious toleration in the shape of the Toleration Act of 1689, regular elections with the Triennial Act of 1694, the ending of pre-publication censorship in England, with the lapsing of the Licensing Act in 1695, and an England of progressive intellectuals, especially John Locke and Isaac Newton.

This interpretation continued with the 1988 tercentenary, when the Revolution was presented as the triumph of the liberal and tolerant spirit, the creation of a political world fit for Englishmen. This interpretation, however, never made much sense from the Scottish or Irish perspective. Moreover, what was for long regarded as an irresistible manifestation of a general aspiration by British society for progress and liberty can now be seen, as it was by contemporaries, as a violent rupture. Thanks to Jacobitism, the succession remained an issue until settled by the victory at Culloden in 1746 of William, Duke of Cumberland, second son of George II.

However, the increased role of Parliament was such that it played a greater part than had been the case under Charles II, let alone James II. In 1689, by the Bill of Rights, Parliament misleadingly declared that James had deserted the kingdom, and also debarred all Catholics from the succession, while, under the Act of Settlement of 1701, the childless Queen Anne was succeeded in 1714 by George, Elector of Hanover, who was descended from James I through the latter's daughter, Elizabeth. Most politics focused on Parliament, and accepted the conventions of a world of elections, votes, political parties and ministries, rather than those of conspiracy and rebellion. If Jacobitism remained a potential challenge, with major risings in Scotland and northern England in 1715–16 and 1745–6, the bulk of politics was less tumultuous. George Lyttelton, then an opposition Whig, in his popular *Letters from a Persian in England* (1735), observed a transformation, from the divided 'enthusiasm' of the religious and political partisanship of the age of Charles I, to a current age in which there was no zeal: 'There is so cold and lifeless an unconcern to everything but a narrow private interest; we are so little in earnest about religion, virtue, honour, or the good of our country'.[1] Lyttelton saw this as a threat to liberty, a theme that was to be taken up by radicals, in Britain and the American colonies, in the 1760s and 1770s.

Britain gains an empire

Parliament also played a role in creating a framework to assist the growth of overseas trade, the spread of trans-oceanic power, and the government of these new territories. Britain had done poorly from the first burst of European trans-oceanic activity at the cusp of the fifteenth and sixteenth centuries. Despite ascertaining the fishing wealth of Newfoundland waters, John Cabot's voyages in 1497–8 were very much on the margins of profitable activity. English expeditions failed to discover the direct route to Asia they sought through a north–west passage to the north of America, or a north–east passage north of Asia, and also missed out on the compensation of American bullion that Cortes and Pizzaro had seized for Spain.

Nevertheless, long-distance seafaring became more important, although storms claimed many lives. In 1600, an East India Company was founded to trade by sea with South and South-East Asia and the East Indies (modern Indonesia), principally in order to obtain spices. This company was eventually to form the basis of Britain's Indian empire.

North America initially seemed a less profitable prospect, but, in 1607, the Virginia Company established a permanent colony at Jamestown, while, in 1620, the *Mayflower* made a landfall at Cape Cod, and the development of a colony in New England began. France, Spain, Sweden and the Dutch were also established in North America. However, the English were successful against them, New Amsterdam becoming New York (named after James, Duke of York, later James II) as a result of conquest from the Dutch. There was a separate, but much less successful, strand of Scottish attempts at colonialisation, notably in Nova Scotia and New Jersey.

There were also English island colonies. Bermuda (1613) was followed by colonies in the West Indies: St Kitts (1624), Barbados (1627) and Nevis (1628). The biggest acquisition, Jamaica, did not follow until 1655, but, by the end of the century, a plantation economy was well developed in the West Indies. It produced sugar for Britain and other European markets, providing the prime source of re-exports; and was worked by slaves brought from West Africa. Britain became the leading power in the slave trade.

Alongside improvements in the availability and use of capital and shipping, and institutional developments, government support for trade and colonies was important. Whereas James I and, even more, Charles I had devoted only limited attention to the colonies, preferring to focus on European power politics, both Cromwell and Charles II saw England as a maritime and commercial power. Navigation Acts sought to control and regulate trade, establishing a clear national preference at the expense of the Dutch, hitherto the more successful maritime and commercial power. At the same time, the British overseas economy benefited from the availability of Dutch capital, and was to do so even more so after the accession of William III in 1689. New colonies were founded in the late seventeenth century, notably Carolina and Pennsylvania, and the pace of migration was such that, by 1700, the population in English North America was considerably greater than that in French North America. The English Atlantic system was stronger than its counterparts in the North Atlantic.

Furthermore, by 1700, England was the leading naval power in the world, while its overseas trade had risen substantially. This increased trade led not only to mercantile prosperity but also to the shifts in diet and fashion seen in such innovations as the import of large quantities of tobacco, coffee, tea and sugar. Economies of scale became the key element, and these required the availability of plentiful capital. London's growing role as a money market was therefore very important to the working of a growing overseas economy, and notably so because the colonies were a region of capital shortage. This pattern remained the case into the twentieth century. Capitalism, in the sense of the creation, mobilisation and direction of capital, was crucial to the development of Britain's global links and, more narrowly, to the ability to make overseas colonies and activity work, and, in particular, work in accordance with the global economy. This capital energised, and was energised by, entrepreneurialism, which was an important element in British society, and notably by the late seventeenth century.

Economies of scale also changed British tastes, particularly with the creation of new consumer fashions. These new fashions drew on the background of a widespread consumerism that was seen in the seventeenth century not only with the purchase of expensive manufactured or imported goods, such as clothes, books and guns, but also with that of more common, lesser-priced goods such as buckles, pins, knitted stockings and starch.

International trade focused on the leading port, London, accentuating its importance in the country: its population rose from 50,000–60,000 in 1500 to 200,000 in 1600 and nearly one million in 1800. In January 1661, the diarist and naval bureaucrat Samuel Pepys took a barge to Blackwall and 'viewed the dock and the new wet dock ... and a brave new merchantman which is to be launched shortly'. Feeding and supplying London's expanding numbers became a key driver of economic activity across much of England. The network of regular carriers' routes focused on London was instrumental in creating a national transport system. Thanks to print, Protestantism and Parliament, London's grasp on the national imagination had become far stronger than in 1650. London very much seemed the source of the high rate of sweeping change across the country and of the words, ideas and images through which change was defined, asserted and debated.

Among the works published there were those about navigation that were significant to British merchants. In 1699–1700, the English astronomer Edmund Halley explored the South Atlantic in the *Paramour*, a war sloop of which he had been given command by William III. Halley's voyages provided information that could be analysed and published. He produced his chart of trade winds in 1689, the first scientific astronomical tables in 1693, and his chart of terrestrial magnetism in 1701, all important tools for navigators.

War with France in 1702–13, the War of the Spanish Succession, brought fresh gains, with Nova Scotia captured and the British position in Hudson Bay and Newfoundland accepted by France. Gibraltar, Minorca and limited rights to trade with the Spanish New World, were gained from Spain. International competition and conflict helped mould the development of government, creating both structural factors and particular pressures, especially those of financing war. This competition also created a context in which domestic circumstances were assessed in terms of relative international effectiveness, notably with regard to France, leading to interest in new institutions, such as the Bank of England in 1694, as well as to periodic reforming bursts.

Parliamentary union with Scotland in 1707 was a key aspect of this process of change. It reflected concerns about the succession, specifically anxiety that England and Scotland would go for different options when Anne died, and tensions over the ability of Scotland to follow a different line in foreign policy. Alongside the security and political dimensions, there were serious economic problems in Scotland. Much of its economy was in a parlous state, and influential circles in Scotland wished to benefit from the economic possibilities of the far larger English market, as well as from those presented by the expanding empire. However, the divisions within Scotland played a major role in the negotiation and passage of Union. Union supporters were largely Presbyterians who were committed to the Revolution Settlement.

The full potential of British overseas power still rested in the future. Conflict with Spain from 1739 to 1748, the War of Jenkins's Ear, and with France from 1743 to 1748, in the War of the Austrian Succession, did not yield anticipated gains in the West Indies and North America, and showed the difficulties of victory. The East India Company did not become an important territorial power in India until after Robert Clive's victory over the Nawab of Bengal at Plassey in 1757, while French Canada was not conquered until 1758–60, Quebec falling in 1759 after James Wolfe's victory outside the city.

Nevertheless, naval dominance had already come to play a greater role in the collective imagination, a process that culminated in 1740 with James Thomson's lines:

> Rule Britannia, rule the waves,
> Britons never will be slaves.

George Frederick Handel's oratorios, such as *Saul*, with their theme of Britain as the modern Israel, a people fulfilling a Biblical patriotism, lent further resonance to this theme of glorious and exceptional destiny. National identity, political system, and maritime character were linked by commentators. John Chamberlayne trumpeted in his *Magnae Britanniae Notitia: or, The Present State of Great Britain* (1726):

> Great Britain may be justly counted the principal nation for trade in the whole world, and indeed the most proper for

trade, being an island which hath many commodious ports and havens, natural products, considerable manufactures, great encouragement from the state for the sake of customs and duties paid, the breeding of seamen, and the increase of shipping, freedom in religion, the pleasure and healthfulness of our clime, the ease and security of our government; all conducing to the encouragement of maritime trade.

This was not a society simply of deference and order, but one in which aristocratic hegemony could also be seen as selfish and disruptive. Yet, it would be misleading to suggest either that there was widespread criticism of the existence of a hereditary hierarchical society, or that tensions were only, or more, apparent between, as distinct from within, social groups. Social tension probably increased after 1760s, but it was not until the crisis in Britain in the 1790s created by the French Revolution that a notion of class-based politics developed. Poaching was a more longstanding testimony to social tension.

The world of ideas

At the same time, other and more profound changes were occurring in the understanding of the world. Science became a major field and source of innovation. In place of the idea that man was only intended to know the mind of God as interpreted by the Church or as found in scriptures, Francis Bacon (1561–1626) popularized the concept that God intended man to recover that mastery over nature which he had lost at Adam's fall from grace. This concept prepared the way for the Scientific Revolution of the late seventeenth century. This saw major advances in discovering the operations of natural laws, particularly the developments in astronomy, mathematics and physics associated with the Royal Society founded in 1660 and with Sir Isaac Newton (1642–1727). His laws of motion offered a coherent system of the universe at once mechanical and mathematically consistent.

Bacon and others offered a challenge to authority but it was transmitted into a new consensus because the Scientific Revolution saw an ability to reconcile new learning with existing élites and their concerns. Building on earlier patterns of court-centred patronage, the Royal Society ensured that science was regarded as contributing to royal *gloire* and to an agenda of progress under monarchical leadership.

A form of science and medicine emerged in which the stress on observation, experiment and careful deduction of laws combined with confidence that knowledge was increasing and better understood. This combination looked toward the modern age, and provided an opportunity for a rethinking not only of the universe but also of the Earth, particularly the world of nature. In this context, human development became different to that of the traditional religious story.

Room for such speculation was provided by the extent to which religious pluralism led not only to tension and sectarianism, but also, eventually, to a degree of toleration, first in fact and then, increasingly, in law. John Locke helped conceive a new view of humanity which allowed diversity in religious views to be recognised as sincerely held opinions, rather than as heresy or sin. Hence toleration replaced persecution (compulsion or condemnation). This idea pervaded eighteenth-century England, leading to religious pluralism and modernity. Most European countries lacked this willingness to accept religious pluralism as other than an unfortunate necessity. The role of the Church in setting truth was replaced by a greater pluralism which provided both opportunities and needs for others to exercise authority or, at least, take a part.

This situation was linked to the political position of the Church of England which was constrained, particularly after the 'Glorious Revolution' to accept a considerable degree of religious freedom for Protestant Nonconformists. This did not mean, however, that the Church lacked support or energy, as was once argued. Instead, there was a considerable degree of conviction in the Church, albeit that the major religious development of the eighteenth century, Methodism, was in part a reaction against established patterns of Anglican devotion and, eventually, became a separate Church.

At the same time as the moves towards the scientific imagination and religious toleration, there was a modernity that looked different to that of standard narratives of modernisation. The new culture of print offered learned treatises, chapbooks, printed ballads and engravings that all commented on witchcraft, with works such as Reginald Scot's *The Discovery of Witchcraft* (1584) and John

Cotta's *The Trial of the Witchcraft* (1616). Belief in the reality of the Devil and of spirits helped ensure that witches also seemed real. In *The Witch of Edmonton* (c. 1621), a play by William Rowley, Thomas Dekker and John Ford, Elizabeth Sawyer, a lonely and bullied old woman, becomes a witch having made a pact with the Devil.

Furthermore, the publications of popular astrologers, such as William Lilly, author of *The Stary Messenger* (1645), sold thousands of copies. The London earthquake of 1692 was seen as a warning of God's anger, an attitude still very much present in the 1750s even though it was also contested by influential commentators. Resort to astrology declined in the eighteenth century, but very large numbers of astrological works were still being sold in the 1790s. Moreover, beliefs in witchcraft, astrology, religious providentialism and, in some lights, science were all seen as aspects of the continuing close interaction of human and sacred space.

This situation could also be seen in literature, much of which addressed the human relationship with the divine. This was seen not only in works explicitly on devotional, philosophical and ethical topics, but also in the world of imaginative literature. Here there were classic themes of sin and redemption and of journeying toward salvation, but also the intervention of the super-human in human life, both past and present. This intervention took a number of forms, as divine judgment, or at least the impact of a purposeful divine Providence and the super-human, manifested itself in different ways. The range not only encompassed the historical and high-drama, but also the 'star-crossed' lovers of romance, as in Shakespeare's *Romeo and Juliet*, and the confusion of mistaken identities repeatedly seen in comedy, as in Shakespeare's *Comedy of Errors*.

Evidence of changing attitudes is provided by growing scepticism, particularly in the eighteenth century, about witchcraft. In Scotland, prosecutions and executions declined after 1662, the last major witch-hunt was in 1697–1700, and the last recorded prosecution was in 1727, and that in Dornoch, which was far distant from the centres of Scottish power and society. There continued to be a popular belief in the existence of witches across Britain. John Wesley (1703–91), the founder of Methodism, believed in ghosts and poltergeists, and was a lifelong collector in his diary of cases of haunting. Nevertheless, there was an increasing tendency to distance and de-personalise the agents of harm.

The reconceptualisation of evil was important not only to a shift in religious sensibility but also to a new understanding of the wider context of human life. A declining emphasis on the direct intervention of Providence and the super-human encouraged a stress on the capacity of humans to mould their environment. There was to be no passive submission to nature. This stress proved an important element in the interest in new outcomes, and determination to prove through new solutions, that was so important not only to the genesis of the Agricultural, Transport and Industrial Revolutions of the eighteenth century but also to the positive response to them.

Sir Isaac Newton's funeral in Westminster Abbey in 1727 was a very grand affair described by Voltaire as that 'of a king who had done well by his subjects'. It was followed by the unveiling of a memorial in Westminster Abbey in 1731. The fame enjoyed by scientists was to be joined later by that of engineers, notably James Watt, again ensuring a distinctive culture of achievement in Britain. The rhetoric accordingly was that of empiricism leading to usefulness, one that linked divine purpose to national strength. The quest to solve the longitude problem at sea was an apt instance, not least as parliamentary legislation in 1714 led to the offering of a prize eventually awarded in 1773. The focus on observation, experimentation and mathematics seen in science provided encouragement for information gathering and the use of data, to help both decision-making and cycles of policy testing and amendment.

The greater understanding of physical laws was to be important in a manufacturing system that benefited from enhanced ways of using objects, notably by pushing, lifting or rotating them. Innovation was revealed as possible and controllable, so that natural resources, notably water, coal and metals, could be used more effectively. Thus, it was possible to devise pumping engines to permit deep mining. Understanding mechanical principles made it easier to employ levers and hydraulics. Science thereby guided and enabled the utilisation of nature's bounty in accordance with Providential design.

CHAPTER FOUR

Britain becomes the world power, 1750–1900

Between 1750 and 1900, Britain became the foremost power in the world, both territorially and in economic terms. An intellectual powerhouse, Britain also became a model political system for much of the world. These changes were interrelated, but the causal relationship is often unclear. Alongside an emphasis on British exceptionalism in change, it is possible to study aspects of the period that did not focus on the debate about change. It is also possible to consider the extent to which developments in Britain, including industrialisation, urbanisation and imperialism, were an aspect of a wider Western process. That was not, however, the general perception in Britain. There was a sense, instead, of the country as distinctive and foremost, and this sense has to be taken into account in assessing its history.

Domestic politics generally takes second place to industrial transformation in any account of the key developments in the period. This emphasis is appropriate given the extent to which this transformation burst asunder the apparent nature of time as cyclical. Instead, industrial transformation made clear that the past would not recur. This transformation suggested, as a result, that arrangements based upon it and legitimated by long usage were no longer valid.

Yet the importance of the politics of the period was that they helped make this transformation possible. Economic change led to major social pressures and large-scale disruption, but there was no serious breakdown in social or political stability. In contrast to many Continental states, there was no revolution in Britain, either at the time of the French Revolutionary crisis at the close of the eighteenth century, or in the mid-nineteenth century when there were revolutions across the Continent. The years 1830 and 1848 were not years of revolution in Britain. This situation did not mean that hardship and discontent were small-scale, but simply that, in a comparative context, they should not be exaggerated.

Economic transformation

Economic transformation was seen in industry, trade, finance, trans-portation and agriculture. The British economy not only changed but also developed powerful advantages in all these respects compared to foreign states. This transformation greatly impressed informed foreign visitors, although they were prone to ignore the impact of industrial depressions, which hit hard at the social welfare system. A culture of improvement lay at the heart of much innovation, and this belief in the prospect and attraction of change moulded and reflected a sense of progress. From 1759, there was a marked increase in the number of patents, which was a testimony to an interest in the profitable possibilities of change. Alongside production, consumption also developed, with the integration of a national market increasingly affecting local production, and with trends in consumption encouraged in newspapers. Consumption helped drive both trade and industrial activity. Commerce indeed was to become a defining characteristic of British society, particu-larly important in townscapes where markets were supplemented and then largely replaced by permanent shops.

The nature of industrial activity also changed, with more specialisation, as well as a greater division of labour and the growth of capital. A greater emphasis on the need for constant, regular and predictable labour led to different forms of labour control, including factory clocks. For rapid industrial growth, the essentials were capital, transport, markets and coal. Coal enabled Britain to avoid the limits of the organic economy, that based on the growth of trees that could be cut down for fuel but the supply of which was limited. Instead, with coal, it was possible to use the plentiful supplies of fossil fuels, supplies that gave Britain a powerful comparative advantage. The use of coal, which had already gathered pace in the sixteenth and seventeenth centuries, fuelling industrial growth, provided a major increase in available energy per head and made possible a rise in per capita living standards. The earlier background was also pertinent in that agricultural developments, whether or not they are presented as an Agricultural Revolution, helped ensure that the same number of people on the land could feed a greatly expanded number who were not engaged in farming, whether or not they worked in industry or commerce in towns or on the land.

Agricultural development in the eighteenth century, including the large-scale use of nitrogenous plants, which enhanced production and land use, as well as the spread of enclosure, ensured that the management of the land was changed. The availability of more food acted as a restraint on the rise in the cost due to an increased population. Agricultural development benefited landowners and their tenants. Although industrial expansion was important, with a major growth in per capita output, agriculture was the principal source of employment and wealth, the most significant sector of the economy, and the basis of the taxation, governmental, ecclesiastical (tithes) and proprietorial (rents) that funded many other activities. Land, and its products, provided the structure of the social system and the bulk of the wealth that kept it in being. Peasant ownership of the land was limited, and land ownership in Britain was relatively concentrated by European standards.

As with transport, industry and other spheres, the emphasis was on improvement. Change was seen as a means of benefit. Thus, with agriculture, new machinery was matched by new crops and by the selective breeding of animals. The emphasis was on the experimental, on developments based on practice, not theory. The application of science was its key element. That aristocrats, such as 'Turnip Townshend' and 'Coke of Norfolk', Charles, 2nd Viscount Townshend, and Thomas Coke, later Earl of Leicester, were happy to devote much time as landlords to improvement was important to the aristocratic culture of the period. Improvement related to agriculture, mining, communications and the development of society and the state.

Coal, a readily transportable and controllable fuel, provided a power source that was more effective than its predecessors: wood and charcoal. Coal, however, had to be mined and transported, and both these requirements acted as spurs for innovation and activity, especially the construction of canals and railways. Faced by the costs of moving coal three miles by packhorse and barge from his colliery at Middletown in Yorkshire to Leeds, Charles Brandling, in 1758, secured an Act of Parliament 'for laying down a wagon-way, in order to the better supplying the town and neighbourhood of Leeds ... with coals', the first Act to authorise the construction of a railway. In 1780, a Newcomen steam engine was installed at Middletown, and, by the close of the century, the pit's average annual output was 78,500 tons.

Steam engines were the icons of the new age. Thomas Jefferson, the future American president, visited the New Albion Mill, a steam-powered flour mill, when he went to London in 1785. He also saw industrial plant in the West Midlands, as well as landscape gardens in southern England. Continued change and the search for improvement were important parts of the process of industri-alisation, and the Newcomen engine was improved, as the casting and boring of cylinders developed, particularly thanks to the new boring machines produced by John Wilkinson in 1774 and 1781. These developments enabled the steam engine to become more efficient in its fuel use and more regular in its operation. In 1769, James Watt (1736–1817), the first to perfect the separate condenser for the steam engine, patented an improved machine that was more energy-efficient and therefore less expensive to run. In 1782, Watt patented further innovations that gave a comparative uniformity of rotary motion, and thus increased the capacity of steam engines to drive industrial machinery.

The application of this potential, a process that fused entrepre-neurship, investment and the freedom to act, was important to industrial development. For example, in 1779, James Pickard, a Birmingham button-manufacturer, fitted a crank and flywheel to his Newcomen engine in order to use its power to drive a mill that could grind metals, an innovation that greatly enlarged the market for steam engines. The *Exeter Weekly Times* of 8 November 1828 referred to 'how rapidly the application of steam power is extending throughout almost every department of the Arts'.

Watt was to be celebrated with a monument in Westminster Abbey, for which the subscription meeting in 1824 was chaired by the Prime Minister, Robert, 2nd Earl of Liverpool. George IV, a conspicuous figure of fashion, gave £500, a twelfth of the sum raised. Other statues to Watt were erected in Glasgow, Manchester, Greenock and Birmingham.

There were also important developments in metallurgy. Coke replaced charcoal for smelting iron and steel. Henry Cort's method of puddling and rolling, invented in 1784, used coal to produce malleable iron more cheaply than the charcoal forge and refinery.

Demand for coal helped to drive transport developments, first canals (including the canalisation of rivers) and then railways. The Sankey Brook Navigation of 1757 carried coal from St Helens to Liverpool, and stimulated both the growth of coal-consuming industries on Merseyside and the expansion of Cheshire's salt industry, which depended on coal-fired salt pans. It was followed by the Duke of Bridgewater's canal, constructed in 1761–7, which took a route independent of any river and was designed to exploit his Lancashire coal mines. Bridgewater followed with the Manchester to Liverpool canal.

Individual developments were important, while the cumulative character of change helped create an impression of transformation. For example, the building of the Staffordshire and Worcestershire Canal between 1766 and 1770 enabled the movement of Staffordshire coal and iron to the River Severn, the first coal barge arrived in Birmingham on the new Birmingham Canal in 1772, and the opening of the Monkland Canal in 1793 stimulated the development of the Lanarkshire coalfield in order to serve the rapidly growing Glasgow market.

Combined with the application of steam power to coal mining, the blast furnaces, and the new rolling and slitting mills, these changes led to a new geography of economic activity. Steam power freed industries from having to locate near riverine sites where water power could be obtained. Instead, industry was attracted to the coalfields, encouraging growth in particular in north-east England, south Lancashire, South Wales and central Scotland, each a region that had earlier had a relatively underdeveloped economy. This underlined the regional character of economic change.

At the local, regional and national levels, the location of new mine shafts, factories and wharves responded to the possibilities of canal transport. When the Britannia Foundry was established in Derby in 1818 to produce quality cast-iron products, it was sited on the banks of the River Derwent, and linked, via that and the

Derby Canal, to the Midlands canal system and the sea. *Smart's Trade Directory* for 1827 noted that from Pickfords' canal wharf in Wolverhampton, a leading centre for the manufacture of iron products, goods could be sent direct to 73 towns including Bristol, Liverpool, London and Manchester. There was a new geography, as landlocked towns, such as Wolverhampton and counties, such as Derbyshire, Staffordshire and Warwickshire, found their relative position transformed. Thanks to the mutually stimulating interaction of waterways and industry, the West Midlands, south Lancashire and South Yorkshire became more important to communications within England.

A new economic geography of resources, production, markets and employment was created. By the 1790s, industrial change had a clear regional pattern that was reflected in indicators such as expenditure on poor relief. Per head, this expenditure was higher in counties with hardly any industry, such as Sussex, or those with declining industries, such as Essex, Norfolk and Suffolk. Indeed, the poverty of such areas was to be a major theme in the early nineteenth century, helping to lead to rural violence, as in the Capital Swing agitation, as well as to emigration.

Regional industrial shifts reflected a range of factors. There was a general crisis of industry in southern England, as coal-based manufacturing encouraged development elsewhere. From the 1780s, the woollen textile industry of the West Riding of Yorkshire acquired a significant price advantage over competitors such as those in Devon, Essex, Norfolk and Worcestershire. More than coal, however, was involved. Labour was cheaper in Lancashire and Yorkshire, and the textile industry less restricted by traditional practices.

The importance of new technology and entrepreneurial energy was demonstrated at Tiverton in Devon where John Heathcoat founded a machine-made net and lace factory. The threat to jobs posed by his patented bobbin net machines had led to the destruction of his Loughborough factory by rioters in 1816, and Heathcoat moved his machines to a disused Tiverton cotton mill. Production from this factory hit lace-making in East Devon, but also showed what could be achieved in the absence of coal. Furthermore, a former partner of Heathcoat, John Boden, opened the Derby Lace Works to the east of Barnstaple in 1825. By 1830, he was employing 1,000 people and, largely as a result, the population of the town rose from 5,079 in 1821 to 7,902 in 1841. The lifestyle and densely inhabited working-class neighbourhood that developed there and in Tiverton was more typical of northern than southern England.

The population rose rapidly in industrial areas: in County Durham, a major centre of coal mining and industry, from about 70,000 in 1700 to 150,000 by 1801. Whereas Scotland and England both averaged annual population increases of 0.3 per cent in 1700–55, between 1755 and 1801 the figure for Scotland was 0.5 and for England 0.8. Furthermore, the link between marriage and childbearing became less powerful, with the recorded illegitimacy rate rising from 1.8 to 5 per cent. On the other hand, marriage became more common and thus normative, and fewer than 9 per cent of people remained unmarried. By 1800, moreover, less of adulthood was now spent in the unmarried state, because the average age at marriage had fallen to 25.5 and 23.7 for men and women respectively. This fall reflected a number of developments that focused on the increased freedom of labour and living arrangements, not least the process by which members of the 'family' withered to 'employees'. For example, farm servants increasingly did not live in with their employers, and thus a restraint on early marriage diminished.

In addition, the rise of urban employment and urban living broke the link between marriage and the availability of land which had been an important restraint on marriage, and notably early marriage. This rise also fostered the social freedom that resulted in more illegitimacy. Marriage rates continued to be affected by real wages, but economic growth in the second half of the eighteenth century created both opportunities and a sense of opportunity that encouraged marriage. Furthermore, infant mortality rates fell in the second half of the eighteenth century. Marital fertility among women aged 35 and over rose from mid-century. This rise was probably the consequence of a fall in stillbirths, and this fall can be seen as evidence of rising average living standards.

The relationship between urbanisation and industrialisation became closer, with the growing cities closely associated with manufacturing or with related commerce and services. On the east coast in the eighteenth century, Sunderland, North and South Shields, Tynemouth and Newcastle all benefited greatly from the export of coal, principally to London, and from coal-based industries, such as glass-making. Shipbuilding became very important in Sunderland and on the Tyne.

Trade was another major cause of population increase. It was particularly significant on the Atlantic coast, principally for Liverpool and Glasgow, each of which benefited from expanding trade with America as well as from the commerce of Empire. The population of Liverpool rose from 83,050 in 1801 to 375,955 in 1851.

Economic growth was even clearer in the comparative dimension, as was urbanisation. The annual average production of coal and lignite, in million metric tons, amounted to 18 for Britain in 1820–4, and 2 for France, Germany, Belgium and Russia, the other leading European industrial powers, combined; and the comparable figures for 1855–9 were 68 and 32. Behind such figures, there was a vivid reality of major change. Dramatic scenes that captured the imagination were reproduced by painters, such as the ironworks in Coalbrookdale, Shropside, with the night illuminated by flaming furnaces. The journalist William Cobbett wrote from Sheffield in January 1830:

> All the way along, from Leeds to Sheffield, it is coal and iron, and iron and coal... Nothing can be conceived more grand or more terrific than the yellow waves of fire that incessantly issue from the top of these furnaces ... it is impossible to behold it without being convinced that ... other nations ... will never equal England with regard to things made of iron and steel... They call it black Sheffield, and black enough it is; but from this one town and its environs go nine-tenths of the knives that are used in the whole world.

In turn, in the world of fiction, which was a major way through which the Victorians viewed the world, novels such as Charles Dickens' *Hard Times* (1854), and Elizabeth Gaskell's *Mary Barton* (1848) and *North and South* (1855), depicted the problems of industrial life, particularly labour disputes and worker misery. Dickens (1812–70) noted the utilitarian, measurement-based, outcome-oriented mentality that industrialisation led to, contrasting, in *Hard Times*, the variety of human experience with this new world: 'So many hundred hands in the Mill; so many hundred horse Steam Power. It is known, to the force of a single pound weight, what the engine will do'.

Dickens saw the emphasis on facts, and on paper information and arguments, as contributing to a deadening distancing from the real nature of social problems. This argument prefigured concerns in our own time that talk of transformation through modern technology has neglected social context and consequences. Like other novelists, including George Eliot and Elizabeth Gaskell, Dickens was also concerned about the need, in the face of the pressure for statistical aggregation arising from rising numbers, to reserve a place for the individual in society. This concern linked the novelists both to the Romantic poets of the 1790s and early nineteenth century and to the Pre-Raphaelite painters of mid-century.

The railway, in which Britain led the world, greatly increased the effectiveness of the country as a manufacturing and marketing system, and thus helped make British industrialisation national in its impact, even if it was highly regional in its character. The progress of the railway was also more generally symptomatic of national development. Wagonways had existed for many years, with horses drawing wagons along rails, especially from collieries to coal-loading quays. The Surrey Iron Railway Company, the world's first railway company and public railway, operated from Wandsworth to Croydon from 1803. Self-propelled steam locomotives changed the situation, not least by making long-distance movement possible. In 1804, Roger Hopkins built a tramroad between Pen-y-darren and Abercynon in South Wales upon which Richard Trevithick tried the first steam railway locomotive engine, essentially a mobile beam engine. The development of the locomotive from the stationery steam-engine provided the technology for the railway revolution, and industrialisation supplied the necessary demand, capital and skills.

George Stephenson opened the Hetton Railway in 1822, the more famous Stockton and Darlington, designed to transport coal to the port of Stockton, following in 1825. Locomotives also improved as part of the cumulative process of development. When Goldsworthy Gurney's steam-jet (or blast) was applied to Stephenson's *Rocket* locomotive in 1829, speeds rose from 16 to 29 miles per hour. Direct drive from the cylinders and pistons to the wheels increased efficiency, as did an engine design that boiled water more rapidly. Railways quickly proved superior to steam coaches which were tried on roads in the 1820s and 1830s.

Railways offered new links and cut journey times for both freight and passengers. They followed the major improvement in roads in the eighteenth and early nineteenth centuries seen with the turnpiking of roads, the enhancement of road surfaces, bridge building, improved carriage construction, and better coach and carrying services. Initially, the railways were mostly small-scale, independent concerns providing local links, and the movement of coal was crucial to their business.

With time, bolder trunk schemes were advanced and financed, and, in addition, already existing lines were linked to create long-distance networks. Services from London reached Birmingham in 1838, Southampton in 1840, and Plymouth in 1847, although the national main-line system was not completed until the early 1870s. Geography was transformed as rivers were bridged, the Menai Strait to Anglesey was crossed in 1849, and tunnels were blasted through hills. About 30,000 bridges were built from 1830 to 1868. Rail was quicker than its competitors and, as a result, canal building stopped in the 1830s.

Furthermore, industries and agriculture were transformed. Use of the railway from the 1840s enabled the brewers of Burton-upon-Trent in Derbyshire to develop a major beer empire, and also helped speed North Wales slates towards urban markets. London newspapers could be transported rapidly round the country. In the 1870s, the railway companies opened up urban markets for liquid milk, encouraging dairy farmers to produce 'railway milk', rather than farmhouse cheese. In 1869, coal brought by sea to London was, for the first time, matched by rail. A decade later, although 6.6 million tons of coal was transported to London by rail, some 3.5 million still entered the Thames by boat.

Thanks to the railway, large numbers travelled at an unprecedented speed and with increased frequency. The impact of rail was also psychological. 'Space' had been conquered. New sounds and sights contributed to a powerful sense of change, and this was overwhelmingly presented as progress, although doubts were raised. In his short story *Dullborough Town* (1860), Dickens presented the train as a cause of lost innocence, as well as a source of new experiences:

Most of us come from Dullborough who come from a country town ... the Station has swallowed up the playing-field. It was gone. The two beautiful hawthorn-trees, the hedge, the turf, and all those buttercups and daisies had given place to the stoniest of jolting roads... The coach that had carried me away, was melodiously called Timpson's Blue-Eyed Maid, and belonged to Timpson, at the coach-office up-street; the locomotive engine that had brought me back, was called severely No. 97 and belonged to SER [South Eastern Railway], and was spitting ashes and hot-water over the blighted ground.

The sense of progress helped to encourage the venture capital that was so important to the expansion of the rail system. Major railway stations, such as Sir Gilbert Scott and W. H. Barlow's St Pancras in London (1873), were designed as masterpieces of iron and glass. They also altered local townscapes and transformed street plans.

Whereas stagecoaches were bumpy, crowded and poorly lit, trains were convenient for reading in. As a result, W. H. Smith and John Menzies developed networks of railway bookstores, helping to create as well as satisfy a new market. The new mass-produced train timetables also provided opportunities for publishers. Samuel Wilberforce, Bishop of Oxford and then Winchester from 1845 to 1873, joked that the book beginning with B that every bishop needed was Bradshaw's, the railway timetable.

In fiction, the train allowed urban sophisticates to take their manners and mores into the countryside, as when Gwendolen Fairfax visits Hertfordshire in Oscar Wilde's play *The Importance of Being Earnest* (1895) and Ethel Henderson comes to Sussex in H. G. Wells' novel *Love and Mr Lewisham* (1900). By train, Sherlock Holmes, and later Hercule Poirot, could descend from London to ferret out villainy, and Scotland Yard detectives could be sent to help provincial police forces.

The railway also brought uniformity as time within Britain was standardised. The railways needed standard time for their timetables in order to make connections possible, and, in place of the variations from east to west in Britain, adopted the standard set by the Greenwich Observatory as 'railway time'. Clocks were kept accurate by the electric telegraph that was erected along lines. The train transformed postal services, with travelling post offices and a system to pick up and drop off the mail at stations without stopping. In 1840, the Penny Black, the world's first postage stamp, was released as part of a system that set a uniform postal rate based on weight in place of a system based on distance. The number of letters delivered in Britain and Ireland rose from 82.5 million in 1838 to 411 million in 1853.

Rail travel itself reflected a social system stratified by wealth. There were three classes, with different conditions and fares. On the London to Brighton line, the third-class carriages lacked roofs until 1852, and were thus exposed to the weather and the hot ash from the engine.

Companies and towns that wished to stay at the leading edge of economic development had to become and remain transport foci. In Carlisle, Jonathan Dodgson Carr adapted a printing machine to cut biscuits, replacing cutting by hand, and, helped by the city's position as a major rail junction, sold his product throughout the country. Machines were increasingly the key, mechanisation bringing profit and larger factories. By 1821, Manchester had over 5,000 power looms, while in Bradford, which became the global centre of worsted wool production and exchange, factory horse-power rose 718 per cent in 1810–30, and the population climbed from 16,012 in 1810 to 103,778 in 1850 by when there were 17,642 automatic looms in Bradford, mass-producing women's dress fabrics.

In the second half of the nineteenth century, industrial growth in Britain increasingly focused on engineering, shipbuilding and chemicals, rather than the textiles and metal smelting of earlier in the century. As industrialisation gathered pace, so did the contrast between industrialised regions and the rest of the country, between, for example, Clydeside and south-west Scotland. The world of work changed. By the mid-nineteenth century, fewer than 10 per cent of those employed in the Scottish central-belt countries of Lanark, Midlothian and Renfrew worked in agriculture, forestry and fishing, although, to feed the growing numbers in industrial areas, there was a major intensification in agricultural activity. This was seen in the enclosure and reorganisation of much land, and in the more intensive use of land, for example as a result of drainage.

The new society

The population of regions experiencing industrial growth rose rapidly. By the 1830s, Glasgow, Liverpool and Manchester each had more than 200,000 inhabitants, and this provided a context for a new reformist politics. The number of people in County Durham rose from 390,997 in 1851 to 1,016,562 in 1891, with a growth of 34.7 per cent alone in the decade 1861–71. In Newcastle, the increase was from 28,294 in 1801 to 215,328 in 1901. Changes in the urban landscape reflected shifts in society. Paintings such as Myles Foster's *Newcastle upon Tyne from Windmill Hill, Gateshead* (c. 1871–2) showed formerly prominent buildings – the castle keep and cathedral, now joined by factory chimneys and the railway bridge.

Major increases in population were only achieved by migration. The dislocation caused by extensive movement of people was part of the pattern of economic growth, essentially to provide labour and yet disruptive for individuals and communities. Areas with limited economic opportunities, such as Cornwall and Ireland, produced large numbers of migrants. Population density, however, rose as the urban population grew, leading to serious overcrowding. This was accentuated by problems created by inadequate water supply and sewage, helping to lead to major epidemics of cholera in 1848–9, 1854 and 1866. Furthermore, indicators such as height, physical well-being, and real earnings suggest that living standards were more generally not rising as fast as growth in leading industrial sectors might suggest. The ravages of famine in Ireland in the 1840s indicated an acute failure in the government's ability to respond adequately to crisis.

Politics 1750–1815

Reform was encouraged by legislative action which increasingly emphasised national standards and institutional provision, but it was also affected by political currents. The rebellion in 13 of the North American colonies in 1775, which led to the Declaration of Independence in 1776 and to a war of independence that lasted until 1783, helped at the time to discredit radicalism in Britain, associating it with national crisis. Subsequently, under William Pitt the Younger, Prime Minister from 1783 to 1801 and 1804 to 1806, defeat in the War of American Independence, and, for long, in the war with France that started in 1793, encouraged pressure for change and revival.

The War of American Independence itself had revealed the limitations of British political and military power. Politically, the difficulty of conceptualising new forms of authority within the existing imperial system had helped lead to breakdown in North America. Alongside the determination of sufficient colonists to go on fighting for independence, the weakness of the army and the crucial failure of naval support in 1781 eventually cost Britain the Thirteen Colonies. However, its capacity for naval power projection allowed it to assure continued control of most of the West Indian colonies despite France (1778), Spain (1779) and the Dutch (1780) joining in the conflict against Britain.

The acceptance of the loss of much of Britain's North American empire with the peace negotiated in 1783 encouraged concern about the viability of the empire as a whole and about Britain's comparative strength. Under Pitt in the 1780s, there was particular interest in fiscal reform.

During the French Revolutionary and Napoleonic Wars (1793–1815), radicalism was discredited as pro-French. In contrast, Throne and Alter ideology became stronger, in reaction to the ideas associated with the French Revolution and its British supporters. At the same time, war encouraged a period of reform designed to enable Britain to meet the challenge from France. Key elements included parliamentary union with Ireland, the establishment of a national census, the extension of the detailed mapping of the country by the Ordnance Survey, the introduction of income tax, and the need to manage the national finances without being on the gold standard.

The length of the struggle against France helped ensure that war, and, more specifically, persistence in the face of adversity, played a key role in national identity. Heroism, particularly the victorious Admiral Horatio Nelson's death at Trafalgar in 1805, and the British infantry squares bravely fighting on under the Duke of Wellington against heavy French attack at Waterloo in 1815, focused a potent sense of meritorious masculinity, imperial destiny, and a quasi-religious trial and salvation.

Reform and monarchy, 1815–37

Personal, as well as national, liberty (a key fusion), nevertheless, remained a crucial definition of national identity, and, after the wars ended, political reform came to be more respectable. However, the strength of Toryism ensured that Robert, 2nd Earl of Liverpool, remained Prime Minister from 1812 until his stroke in 1827. Indeed, the continuance of the Tory interest seemed foreordained, Lord Byron writing in *Don Juan* that:

> Nought's permanent among the human race,
> Except the *Whigs* not getting into place.

In practice, the Tory order collapsed in the early 1830s. From the 1830s, as reform became more self-conscious as a political cause, in both Church and State, there was a habit of denouncing 'old corruption' and of attacking the pre-Reform political system as corrupt and the pre-Reform government as incompetent. These charges, however, were inaccurate, and sprang from partisanship and a failure to understand the character, political culture, and achievements of pre-Reform Britain. Alongside complacent clerics, there were others (the majority), who ministered energetically to their flocks. Furthermore, most government functions were discharged within the conventions of the period.

Whatever the pressure for reform, hostility to the political order was far from universal. The Exeter-based *Western Luminary and Family Newspaper*, for example, attacked 'a spirit of insubordination and discontent' in its issue of 4 January 1831. Many would have agreed with this Tory and Church newspaper. Indeed, Henry Philpotts, who had been consecrated Bishop of Exeter two days earlier, voted against the Reform Bill and in October 1831 clashed in the House of Lords with the Whig Prime Minister, Charles, 2nd Earl Grey. Philpott's opposition to reform led to violence in Exeter, with his son using coastguards to garrison the episcopal palace against an attack by local radicals. Despite major pro-reform riots in Bristol and Nottingham, there was no comparison with the unsuccessful conspiracy in the West Country that had formed part of the Jacobite plan for an insurrection in 1715.

The shift in political culture away from violence had left a lasting impact, although economic transformation continued to be the cause of a strand of violence that could have a radical political dimension. This linked the Peasants' Revolt of 1381 and the anti-enclosure risings of the sixteenth and early seventeenth century to the opposition to new machinery in the early nineteenth, including the Luddite protests of the 1810s against industrial machines, and their later Captain Swing counterparts against agricultural machines.

Crucially, for the politics of the 1820s and 1830s, monarchy responded positively if reluctantly to the new challenges, rather than, as across much of the Continent, for example France, Spain and Austria in the 1820s, championing the cause of reaction. This stance was important to the definition of British conservatism as a movement able to respond to tendencies and repeatedly to shun the appeal of ultra (ultra-conservative) positions in favour of a commitment to practicalities.

The monarchs of the period are of great interest. George IV (r. 1820–30) is best remembered in terms of his stately and very expensive pleasure dome, the Brighton Pavilion, as well as for his self-indulgence and womanising, which were the themes of satirical cartoonists; but there was far more to him and his rulership. In particular, he expanded the range of the monarchy in the most vivid way by letting himself be *seen*. George was determined that his coronation, held on 19 July 1821, should be a lavish spectacle, and he planned the ceremony accordingly. The staging was carefully prepared, and, in a major affirmation of conservative values, Parliament granted £240,000 to meet the costs – a marked contrast with the £70,000 spent on George III's coronation. The royal crown was enhanced by an unprecedented number of borrowed jewels, so that 12,532 diamonds were used in the setting. The impact was somewhat tarnished when George's estranged wife, Caroline, whose demand for crowning had been rejected, was refused entry at the Abbey, and the door shut in her face. Nevertheless, the general public response was favourable, and the coronation helped foster public loyalty. This was taken forward by George's visits to Ireland, Hanover and Scotland. These visits are important as they indicate the variety of roles facing the monarchy as it adapted to a rapidly changing society.

The eighteenth-century monarchs had not visited Scotland or Ireland. The Parliaments of Edinburgh and London were united under Anne, without her, or any of her successors, visiting Scotland; those of Dublin and London were united under George III, without him or indeed any of his sons during his reign visiting Ireland. Conquest had led monarchs and princes to travel – William III to Ireland in 1690 and William, Duke of Cumberland to Culloden Moor in 1746 – but George IV went for different reasons.

It was instructive that George visited Ireland first. Its population was larger than that of Scotland, Wales or Hanover, and, as a result of parliamentary Union, which came into effect in 1801, Ireland was also important not only in its own right but also in the Westminster Parliament for what was now the United Kingdom of Great Britain and Ireland. The Parliaments of London and Dublin were joined as those of London and Edinburgh had been in 1707. This union followed the suppression of an Irish rising and the defeat of a French invasion, both in 1798. The Union with Ireland lacked the logic of a shared Protestantism and the lubricant of economic transformation that were to ensure that that with Scotland worked until the early twenty-first century. However, although strained from the outset, it was far from inevitable that the Union would fail and indeed it was not to do so until in the very different circumstances of the years after World War One.

Soon after returning from Ireland, George set off for Hanover, where he was rapturously greeted by his Hanoverian subjects. This was the first visit by a King of Hanover to his dominion and it indicated a direction that an Anglo-Hanoverian monarchy could have taken.

Another commitment was met by George's visit to Scotland in 1822. His wearing of Highland dress of an especially lavish type was particularly successful in courting popularity. At the same time, the Highlandism of the visit sent a fairly unsubtle message that Jacobitism was now equated with loyalism, and that therefore the erstwhile opponents of Hanover could now defend the cause of Toryism, social stability and opposition to Reform, the cause dear to George. What George made of the sermon he heard preached by the Moderator of the Church of Scotland, against lust and in favour of marital harmony, is unknown; but he was accustomed to the consequences of his position as a public defender of the moral order. Favouring Scottish music, dances and drinks, such as Glenlivet and Atholl Brose, strikes a very modern note, and, as a sign of changing technology, George's yacht the *Royal George* was assisted in the face of contrary winds by steam tugs. The age of the royal tour was here, and in Scotland George ably aligned himself with the possibilities of Romantic nationalism. In 1824, he also showed his concern for national development when he gave a twelfth of the sum raised for the monument in Westminster Abbey to James Watt.

More conservative as he aged, George, like his father, opposed Catholic Emancipation – votes for Catholics – and in 1828 insisted that the government should not support it. The Prime Minister, the Duke of Wellington, the victor at Waterloo, however, saw Emancipation as necessary, not least in order to integrate Ireland into what had become the United Kingdom, and pressed George hard. The angry King threatened ·abdication, but finally agreed in 1829 to sign the Catholic Relief Act, which introduced Emancipation. George's willingness to bow to necessity defined this last stage of his reign, and, however unenthusiastic, was an important move towards a non-confessional state, in other words one no longer dominated by the position and interests of the Church of England.

The defeat of Napoleon at Waterloo had been followed by the restoration of the Bourbons to the throne of France in the person of the pear-shaped Louis XVIII. In 1830, however, his brother, the conservative Charles X, was overthrown by revolution. It was unclear whether Britain would also rebel. Reform demands produced bitter riots in Bristol, Derby and Nottingham in 1831 as Parliament debated plans for altering the electoral system: both the right to vote and the distribution of parliamentary constituencies. This was the crisis that faced William IV (r. 1830–7), the third son of George III; the second, Frederick, 'the Grand Old Duke of York', had already died.

Temperamentally, William, although not as conservative as George IV, was not in favour of major change, and he was hostile to radicalism, but William wanted to be a constitutional monarch, wished to keep the peace, and was willing to accept pressure for a new electoral system from the Whig Party. The general election that resulted from William's accession (parliaments then came to an end with each reign) was followed in November 1830 by the defeat of the Tory government under Wellington, who had declared his opposition to parliamentary reform. A Whig government under Earl Grey followed. Grey, whose memory is celebrated in the Grey Monument in the centre of Newcastle, supported reform not least because he feared that, without it, there would be a revolution, as in France, Belgium and across most of Italy. The Reform Bill, however, was defeated at the Committee stage in April 1831.

Grey then sought a dissolution of Parliament, preparatory to a new election designed to lead to a more reform-minded Commons. William's agreement to this dissolution, and thus to the second general election in quick succession, was very popular among supporters of reform. He could, instead, have refused another election and sought to appoint another Prime Minister, but William was not by temperament a reactionary.

The second Reform Bill passed the Commons in September 1831, after the general election had returned Grey with a very large majority, but it was thrown out by the Tory-dominated House of Lords. While the prospects of a compromise Bill were probed in discussions, there was much popular agitation, including bitter riots. A third Reform Bill, which reflected modifications arising from the recent discussions, was introduced in the Commons in December 1831, passing its second reading with a large majority. The attitude of the Lords, however, remained crucial and it was unclear that the modifications would ensure sufficient support. The King was asked to appoint enough peers to secure the success of the Bill. William, who respected the position of the House of Lords, and was worried about the content and tendency of the Reform Bill, as well as by Grey's inability to distance his policy from that of the radical Whigs, nevertheless felt that he had to support the government. Reluctantly, he agreed to create enough peers to support the passage of the Bill in the Lords, if such a course was necessary, and also to press the peers to pass the measure. The creation of peers in such a fashion had last occurred over a century earlier, under Queen Anne, when 12 peers had been created in 1711 to ensure the passage of the Treaty of Utrecht which, in 1713, brought to an end Britain's participation in the War of the Spanish Succession.

Having passed its third reading in the Commons, the Bill went to the Lords, but met with defeat on an amendment on 7 May. Grey then asked William for 50 new peers and when William, who had only been thinking of about 21, refused, he resigned. William turned to the Tories, but Tory divisions ensured that they could not offer an alternative. This obliged William, who did not wish to see another general election, and the disruption and uncertainty that would cause, to turn to Grey and to accept the need to create peers as he wished. Rather than doing so, however, William was responsible for a circular letter to Tory peers that led many to decide to abstain, as Wellington promised to do. Under this pressure, the Lords yielded.

When it came to the crunch, the King had been led to back Grey by the widespread support for reform, by the view that the choice was between reform and widespread disorder, but also, in the crisis created by Tory divisions, by Grey's opposition to further changes, and by the sense that the Reform Bill would not be followed by a total transformation of British politics. In fact, what became the First Reform Act was a major change to both franchise and political geography. The English electorate increased by 50 per cent, so that about one-fifth of all adult males could vote. The distribution of seats was radically altered with information employed to produce a rational system. The 'Drummond Scale' ranked parliamentary boroughs on criteria including the population, the number of houses they contained, and the amount of assessed taxes paid.

Representation was taken away from rotten boroughs with few voters, in order to reward growing towns, such as Birmingham, Blackburn, Bolton, Bradford, Leeds, Manchester, Oldham, Sheffield and Sunderland, that had not, hitherto, had their own MPs. Separate Acts were also passed for Ireland and Scotland. The Act helped underline the extent of popular representation through the electoral system, and thus sustained the broad popular acceptance of the political system. It led to a relative increase in the political importance of the north of England, itself the industrial centre of the country; and this created a dynamic of change in the political system.

William's role in reform assured his popularity, Grey telling the Lords when his niece Victoria succeeded him in 1837, 'if ever there was a Sovereign entitled to the character, his Majesty may truly be styled "a Patriot King!"'. In the caricature *The Reformers' Attack on the Old Rotten Tree*, which advocated electoral reform, William was portrayed on 'Constitution Hill', applauding the process of reform. In the caricature *The Balance of Power in 1831*, the Whigs were depicted sitting on the lower end of the seesaw, which was weighted down by the Crown and the press, most prominently the *Times*, while the Tories were up in the air. The contrast between the large number of pubs named after William and the small number named after George IV is instructive.

Victorian politics and society

When Victoria, a beautiful young 18-year-old, succeeded to the throne in 1837, she was the first unmarried woman to do so since Elizabeth Tudor in 1558. Like Elizabeth, Victoria's route to the throne was a complex one, which reflected the vagaries of dynastic politics. Unlike with the Tudors, however, there were no executions to mark the route. The chance of a daughter born to George III's fourth son succeeding to the throne might have seemed as remote as that of the Hanoverian dynasty acceding in 1714, but, as so often in these cases, death and infertility blazed the path for the outsider. Although there were many bastards, especially the ten of William, Duke of Clarence, later William IV, and the actress Dorothy Jordan, there were only three legitimate children born to George III's eldest three sons, George IV, Frederick, Duke of York and William IV. George IV's daughter, Charlotte, however, died in 1817, a few hours after she gave birth to a stillborn son, while the two daughters born to Adelaide, the wife of the future William IV, both died in infancy.

Because of these deaths, Victoria, the daughter of Edward, Duke of Kent, who had died in 1820, was therefore a great catch. The lucky princeling, Albert of Saxe-Coburg-Gotha, his case pushed hard by his uncle, the influential Leopold, King of the Belgians, was a happy case of dynastic choice becoming love-match, and the couple was married in 1840. Victoria had chosen him against the wishes of her mother. He was an ardent husband whose life with Victoria was surprisingly passionate for those who think that Victorian values mean sexual repression.

Rapidly educating himself in the details of the British political system, Albert emphasised the need for the Crown to adopt political neutrality, and helped lessen Victoria's partisan preference for the Whig ministry of Lord Melbourne, a necessary task as, under its leader Sir Robert Peel, Tory popularity revived. Crucially,

Albert did his dynastic duty by fathering many children, and thus avoiding the danger of the unpopular Ernest, Duke of Cumberland, George III's fifth son and Victoria's uncle, being next in line for the British throne. Because Hanover did not accept female succession, Ernest had become King of Hanover in 1837.

Albert was also active in a host of spheres across public life. His prestige, drive and tact helped make him a sound committee man, and, through his position as the chairman of committees, he helped drive forward the cause of national improvement. Thus, after Parliament burned down, Albert was appointed as Chairman of the Royal Commission that was formed to choose frescoes to decorate the inside of the new Parliament buildings. He supported using the rebuilding as an opportunity to promote British arts.

More dramatically, he played a major role, not least as President of the Society for Arts from 1843, in promoting the Great Exhibition held in Hyde Park in 1851. In 1846, he told a deputation that 'to wed mechanical skill with high art is a task worthy of the Society of Arts and directly in the path of its duty'. In contrast, George IV had sponsored high art, but not mechanical skill.

The Great Exhibition was seen as an opportunity to link manufacturing and the arts, in order to promote a humane practicality in which Britain would be foremost and from which the British people and economy could benefit. The Exhibition itself was a tremendous feat of organisation, a secular cathedral of cast iron and glass, and the first wonder of the modern world. It reflected an attempt to embrace and to channel industry, the new Britain. This attempt in part arose from Albert's visit to Birmingham in 1843, an affirmation of a link between monarchy, industry and modernity which took forward George III's interest in canal construction and manufacturing processes. Due to radical agitation, Albert was advised not to visit the city, but he did so, touring five major factories and being favourably received.

Albert was a self-conscious moderniser, willing to work hard in order to acquire the detailed knowledge necessary to understand how best to implement change successfully. He was a practical paternalist, keenly committed to improvement and concerned to lessen social discontents, an attitude much in line with reform opinion. In 1848, the year in which governments across Europe were swept aside by revolutions, and in which Chartist demands for change unsuccessfully challenged the British system, Albert made his views clear when he spoke at a meeting of the Society for Improving the Condition of the Working Classes, arguing that the wealthy had a duty to help, that progress would not come from revolution, and that 'any real improvement must be the result of the exertion of the working people themselves'. He was committed to public health and policing, both of which were greatly developed in mid-century, as reform led to new institutions and the standardisation of provision.

Chartism was a large-scale protest movement of the 1830s and 1840s which pressed, in the Six Points of the People's Charter, for universal adult male suffrage, a secret ballot, annual elections, equal parliamentary constituencies, the abolition of property qualifications for MPs and their payment. The Second Chartist Petition, a demand for reform, rejected by Parliament in 1842, noted: 'The borough of Guildford with a population of 3,902 returns to Parliament as many members as Tower Hamlets with a population of 300,000', the latter figure a testimony to the enormous expansion of the East End. Chartism's appeal was varied. In London, the poor saw Chartism largely as a movement against taxes that hit them hard.

Many of Chartism's ideas, including democratic accountability, influenced popular Liberalism from the 1850s. There was a growth in interest in the working class building up its own institutions, such as a multitude of friendly societies and clubs, and in schemes for improving the physical and moral condition of working people through education and temperance.

Despite the failure of Chartism, officially sanctioned reform was a major theme and its range was considerable. The Factory Acts of 1833, 1844, 1847, 1850, 1860 and 1874 regulated conditions of employment, the Poor Law Amendment Act of 1834 standardised poor relief, and the County and Borough Police Act of 1856 made the formation of paid police forces obligatory, taking forward the County Police Act of 1839.

Control was a major theme. Thus, the New Poor Law brought those in need of support into workhouses, often a grim option. Much of the regulatory structure of modern Britain, prior to the introduction of European norms in recent decades, dates from this period. For example, the introduction of the civil registration of births, marriages and deaths in 1837 lessened the role of the established Church, while state responsibility for elementary education was introduced in 1839.

Health problems also helped lead to an impressive effort, including large-scale investment in public works. In 1848, the Public Health Act created a General Board of Health and an administrative structure to improve sanitation, especially water supply. The new Act provided for the creation of local boards of health, and they took action. For example, the Board of Health established in Leicester in 1849 was instrumental in the creation of a sewerage system and in tackling slaughterhouses and smoke pollution. A critical report on Derby by Edward Cresy, a super-intending inspector under the General Board of Health, led the Liberal councillors to embark on a programme of works, including public baths and washhouses.

This was part of a more widespread process of activism which was particularly important in altering the urban landscape and which helped to counter the worse ravages of social distress, as well as to introduce a broader pattern of improvement. Activism combined local initiatives and central supervision administered by inspectors, and the latter was a part of a major shift in the character of British government.

Pressure for public regulation brought into dispute competing notions of governmental responsibility, namely duty of care versus *laissez faire*, the latter held to be a matter of freedom and a cause of economic growth. In this politicised and value-rich environment, the British government moved towards regulation. It expanded its scope through advancing the claims of reform, and was expected to do so, notably by commentators. For example, in 1851–4, the *Lancet*, the leading medical periodical, under its radical editor Thomas Wakley (1795–1862), published a series of reports from the Analytical Sanitary Commission attacking the adulteration of food and drink. In turn, this pressure led to a Parliamentary Select Committee in 1855 and to legislation in 1860 which began modern food regulation in Britain.

With its population rising from just over one million in 1801 to over seven million by 1911, London, the capital of *the* world empire, presented the most serious problem, but, from 1859, under the direction of Joseph Bazalgette, Chief Engineer to the Metropolitan Board of Works, a drainage system was constructed. Fully completed in 1875, this contained 82 miles of intercepting sewers that took sewage from earlier pipes that had drained into the Thames, and transported it to new downstream works.

Pumping stations with Cornish beam engines provided the power. Storm-relief sewers followed in London in the 1880s. Combined with the new underground railway, this ensured a new subterranean architecture that reflected the ability of engineers to extend, as well as alter, the built environment.

More modest townscapes were also transformed in the name of utility, propriety, convenience and reform. This included the removal of markets from town streets to purposely built market houses, as in Tiverton in 1830 and Crediton in 1836. Honiton High Street lost its shambles in 1823. Timber and thatch were seen as dated, unattractive, non-utilitarian and, increasingly, non-urban. Urban facilities and functions grew. Exeter's first bank was opened in 1769 and its first gasworks in 1817, and the four city gates were removed from 1769 to 1819. Paving was extended to existing thoroughfares, as in Tiverton under an Act of 1794.

The new society of urbanisation and industrialisation created other novel needs. The development of urban working-class leisure, away from traditional customs and towards new mass, commercialised interests, was one of the responses to the changing society. Music-halls and football clubs were founded in large numbers. The Recreation Grounds Act of 1859 and the Public Health Act of 1875 encouraged the laying out of public parks. Municipal parks and buildings testified to the strength of local identity and to the desire and ability to improve the local environment.

Standardisation and regulation extended to the right to vote in national elections in 1832 (the First Reform Act), and in borough elections in 1835 (the Municipal Corporations Act). Under the Second Reform Act of 1867, rate-paying male householders in boroughs gained the vote, while, in 1884, the Third Reform Act extended this franchise to the boroughs, the first time that the country had been brought under the same electoral system. Women, however, did not gain the vote until 1918 and, on an equal basis, until 1928. The democratisation of local government followed, with Local Government Acts in 1888 and 1894.

Although there were tactical and other differences, Liberal and Conservative governments both supported reform, the Second Reform Act being a Conservative measure, as was the 1888 Local Government Act. Under William Gladstone, the Liberal leader, the 1870 Education Act divided the country into school districts under education boards and stipulated a certain level of educational provision, a key step in a process that led to spreading literacy; while open competition was introduced into the civil service in 1870 and the secret ballot established for elections in 1872. Under his Conservative counterpart, Benjamin Disraeli, legislation in 1874–5 systematised and extended the regulation of important aspects of public health and social welfare, while the Prison Act of 1877 established state control. As an instance of the general process, in 1876 the Unseaworthy Ships Act ensured that ships carried a Plimsoll line: a horizontal marking giving the point beyond which the ship was overladen and it was therefore illegal for it to sail.

As government became more activist and regulatory, so the goal of the political groupings that controlled it increasingly became that of seizing the opportunity to push through policy, as much as office-holding for personal profit and prestige. The nature of power within society was now discussed to a greater extent than a century earlier. The large-scale popular petitions against the Corn Laws in the 1830s and 1840s reflected widespread interest in, and commitment to, key issues in public economy.

More generally, the expanding middle class expected power and status, and was dubious of established institutions and practices that did not seem reformist or useful. Deference was eroded and inherited privilege that lacked purpose was criticised. The Conservative Party became a body defending property rather than social privilege. Middle-class views and wealth stimulated a demand for, and process of, improvement, civic and moral, that was central to the movement for reform.

This process had an echo in the world of the novel, where attitudes were grounded in a popular and readily comprehensible format. Dickens' novels reflected many of the anxieties of mid-Victorian society, and echoed calls for reform. Thus, *Little Dorrit* (1855–7) was an attack on aristocratic exclusiveness, bureaucratic administrative methods and imprisonment for debt.

'Morality' and reform agitation were not only middle-class causes. Self-improving artisans were also involved, and their support was sought by the political parties. At the same time, hierarchy and deference remained very pronounced in some spheres, not least in the presence and treatment of servants. In *He Knew He Was Right* (1868–9), the industrious novelist Anthony Trollope depicted the debilitating pressure of service. The snobbish, religious, reactionary, spinster Jemima Stanbury 'kept three maid-servants ... But it was not every young woman who could live with her. A rigidity as to hours, as to religious exercises, and as to dress, was exacted, under which many poor girls altogether broke down; but they who could stand this rigidity came to know that their places were very valuable'.

Nevertheless, rising pressure towards the end of the century for women to receive a fairer deal, and for women's interests as a separate question not to be answered by reference to the past, challenged conventional assumptions. The suffragette movement, notably the Women's Social and Political Union, led by the Pankhursts, which sought to force public attention onto the issue of extending voting rights to women, was a prominent aspect of a more general articulate and public challenge to gender roles. On the one hand, the practical impact of the idea of the 'new woman' is easily overstated, even for middle-class (let alone working-class) women. Instead, the idea of separate spheres, with women running the home and family, displayed both resilience and adaptability. Moreover, in the world of work, women mostly moved into the low-skill, low-pay 'sweated' sector, and were generally worse treated than men, a practice in which the trade unions co-operated with the management.

Nevertheless, there was an incremental process of change. Whereas the London Government Act of 1899 excluded women from the vote for the new metropolitan boroughs, in 1907 another Act gave women the vote in local elections. Opportunities for women increased in the universities. For example, they were admitted to London degrees in 1878.

More generally, it was no longer a case of change affecting society, politics, the economy and culture. Instead, change became integral to their structures and, in part, ethos. This challenged all institutions and was unsettling to much of the population. The varied manifestations of this unease included hostility to immigrants and a wider disquiet about the state of the nation. This disquiet encouraged social analysis, notably by Henry Mayhew, Charles Booth and Seebohm Rowntree, calls for public action and charitable missions.

The world's greatest empire

While such missions surveyed and provided help to the East End of London, a comparable process was at work across the Empire, which was increasingly, in Britain, justified in terms of moral purposes, including social improvement, economic progress, enlightenment and Christianisation. This, however, was not the root-cause of this expansion. Instead, war and international competition led to Britain becoming the world's leading empire. Thanks to repeated naval victories in the war with France in 1793–1815, culminating with Nelson's victory against a larger Franco-Spanish fleet at Trafalgar in 1805, Britain was left free to execute amphibious attacks on the isolated colonial centres of non-European powers, and also to make gains at the expense of non-European peoples.

The Congress of Vienna (1814–15) recognised this success, and Britain retained her control of Cape Colony, the Seychelles, Mauritius, Trinidad, Tobago, St Lucia, Malta and Ceylon (Sri Lanka). Most of the trans-oceanic European imperial world in the eastern hemisphere was British, and the collapse of the Spanish-American empire was to ensure that by 1830 this was true of the entire world. Britannia ruled far more than just the waves. The symbol of this power was Nelson's Column, erected in 1843, which dominated much of London prior to the age of the skyscraper, serving as a secular counterpoint to St Paul's Cathedral. Hitler regarded the column as 'the symbol of British naval might and world domination', and planned to take it as war booty to his capital, Berlin.

To criticise contemporary attitudes to Empire (like social conditions or the treatment of women in Britain), as if Britain could have been abstracted from the situation elsewhere, is unhelpful and, in a profound sense, like much criticism of the Victorian period, ahistorical. Within the constraints of the technologies and attitudes of the age, the British were more liberal than other major European powers. Britain offered a powerful support to the struggles for independence in Latin America and Greece, from Spanish and Turkish rule respectively, and the British were instrumental in ending the slave trade and slavery, despite the economic damage done to the colonies in the West Indies. The Act for the Abolition of the Slave Trade (1807) reflected the strength of the moral strand in

British public life. This strand drew greatly on the world of public discussion that reached through the press and public collections and meetings into every hamlet. Anti-slavery literature was prolific and struck both evangelical and providential notes and also, as in Thomas Clarkson's *The Substance of the Evidence of Sundry Persons on the Slave Trade* (1788), those of an informed pragmatic discussion of issues. Britain was also the home to émigrés and those fearing repression abroad, such as Karl Marx.

Territorial expansion provided raw materials, markets and employment, and, combined with evangelicalism, encouraged a sense of Britain as at the cutting edge of civilisation. Indeed, Empire was in part supported on the grounds that it provided opportunities for the advance of civilisation, not least by ending what were seen as uncivilised as well as unchristian practices, such as widow-burning and ritual banditry in India. The country's destiny increasingly appeared imperial and oceanic. British capital and expertise also played a major role in many parts of the world.

In the second half of the century, the British fought across the world as never before. None of these conflicts was a war for survival or transformed British society, but their cumulative impact for Britain was important, not least in encouraging the view that its destiny was as a great imperial power; and their individual impact on other societies was formative. Britain's role was part of the wider story of European imperialism, but greater than that of any other state, because of her limited part in European power politics, her unprecedented naval and commercial strength, and the already extensive character of the Empire.

The British Empire was far larger, in area and population, than that of any other power. The Empire focused on India, the most populous part and the basis of much of its power, particularly its ability to act as a force on land. The Empire also saw major expansion in Africa and, with less resistance, in Australasia. Enemies the British fought included the Russians, the Chinese, Indian opponents and rebels, the Maori of New Zealand, the Afghans, and, in Africa, the Asante, the Zulu, the Mahdists of Sudan and the Boers (Afrikaners) of southern Africa. There were defeats, such as Isandlwana at the hands of the Zulu in 1879, and a series of humiliating failures in the opening stage of the Second Boer War (1899–1902). However, the British military proved able to respond to challenges, and was helped by naval dominance, superior firepower, and the ability to deploy significant resources. Invading Sudan in 1896, the British built a railway straight across the desert from Wadi Halfa to Abu Hamed. Extended to Atbara in 1898, it played a major role in the supply of the British forces. The Zulu and the Boers were overcome in the end.

In the 1870s, two Empires had been proclaimed. In 1871, the King of Prussia, Wilhelm I, whose son had married Victoria's daughter, became Emperor of Germany, presiding in that role over lesser German monarchies such as Bavaria and Saxony. The Second Reich or Empire (the first was the medieval Holy Roman Empire abolished in 1806 as Napoleon reshaped Europe), would last until it was defeated in 1918. More surprisingly, Victoria, the Widow of Windsor, five years later, in 1876, became Empress of India – an empire that was to last until the sub-continent was granted independence in 1947.

Imperial status was part of the re-creation of Victoria. She was coaxed from reclusive widowhood to a new public role by her Prime Minister, Benjamin Disraeli, a novelist turned-Tory politician, who combined imperial policies with social reform and who sought to foster a sense of national continuity. He realised that monarchy was a potent way to lead the public and control the consequences of the spread of the right to vote in Britain. This view was gently mocked in W. S. Gilbert and Arthur Sullivan's comic operetta *The Pirates of Penzance* (1879), in which the victorious pirates at once surrender when summoned to do so in the name of the Queen. Disraeli carefully manipulated Victoria into accepting his view and playing the goal he had allocated her. Disraeli was a warm, although not uncritical, supporter of Victoria. At once an opportunistic and skilful political tactician, who was also an acute thinker, Disraeli was able to create around the themes of national identity and pride, and social cohesion, an alternative political culture and focus of popular support to the Liberal moral certainty in which Disraeli's rival, William Gladstone, flourished.

There was another problem of authority and governance with which the monarchy could help, that of Empire. Under the Queen-Empress, the British Empire expanded as never before, so that, by 1900, 400 million were her subjects. Reginald, 12th Earl of Meath, launched and financed Empire Day, celebrated on 24 May, Victoria's birthday, although it was not officially endorsed by the government until 1916. Streets, towns, geographical features and whole tracts of land were named or renamed in Victoria's honour, including the Australian state of Victoria, the city of Victoria on Vancouver Island in Canada, Victoria Falls on the River Nile, and a major railway station in London, matching Waterloo.

The British monarchy was important, however, not only as a treasury of place names. It also helped provide a political system for the government of much of the world, a system that matched the extension of liberty seen in Britain, and a system that in some respects and in certain colonies was very modern, with its extension of liberties and delegation of powers.

The government of Empire was very varied. In some colonies, there was straightforward imperial rule by representatives of the British state, often authoritarian and militaristic. In India, however, there was a careful attempt to incorporate existing hierarchies, interests and rituals. There, the princely dynasties that had gained effective independence with the decline of the Mughal Empire in the eighteenth century, only to be overawed by the British, were wooed from the 1870s by the creation of an anglicised princely hierarchy that gave them roles and honours, such as the orders of the Star of India and the Indian Empire, in accordance with British models and interests. This process was also to be followed in Malaya and in parts of Africa.

The result was a stress on status, not race, that is easy to criticise, not least because an emphasis on inherited privilege served as a brake on inculcating values of economic, social and political development. Nevertheless, this policy was also a response to the large amount of India that had been left under princely rule, and helped strengthen the British position and consolidate the 'internal frontier' of imperialism. Furthermore, the search for support in India and elsewhere was a multi-layered one, extending to the co-option or creation of professional and administrative groups able to meet local as well as imperial needs.

In the settlement colonies, the long-established colonies of white settlement, self-government was extended from the mid-nineteenth century with the growth of what was called responsible government. This meant that, in another major measure of liberalisation, colonial governors were to be politically responsible to locally elected legislatures, rather than to London, a process that reflected the institutionalising of the comparable parliamentary arrangement in Victorian Britain. This system was first applied when Québec and Ontario were joined together in the Province of Canada in 1841; a capital was chosen at Bytown (Ottawa) in 1857, and the Parliament there drew on the neo-Gothic example of the new Houses of Parliament in Westminster. Other colonies followed on the path of responsible government: Nova Scotia in 1848, Prince Edward Island in 1851, New Zealand in 1852, New Brunswick in 1854, Newfoundland, New South Wales, Victoria, Tasmania and South Australia in 1855, Queensland in 1859, the Cape in 1872, Western Australia in 1890, and Natal in 1893.

Dominion status took this process further, offering a peaceful, evolutionary route to independence. Canada became a Dominion in 1867, Australia in 1901, and New Zealand in 1907. Although the Colonial Laws Validity Act of 1865 declared colonial legislature that clashed with that from Westminster invalid, the Act was only rarely invoked. The Act echoed the 1720 Declaratory Act, but Westminster did not push as hard with the Dominions as with Ireland to subordinate their parliaments.

This was a federalism that worked. During the Boer War in southern Africa in 1899–1902, the Empire, particularly Australia, Canada, Cape Colony and New Zealand, sent troops, which fostered Dominion nationalism within the Empire, rather than having it as a separatist force. Meetings of prime ministers from 1887 helped give the Dominions a voice in imperial policy and also offered a means for coherence. They were prefigured from 1867 by the Lambeth Conferences of colonial bishops, which provided a system of consultation that helped support the continued acknowledgement of the spiritual authority and leadership of Archbishops of Canterbury. More powerfully, the Crown provided a crucial cohesion for Empire, at once symbolic but also an effective source of identity and sustainer of loyalty.

Victoria's willingness to make conciliatory gestures to other creeds was important in this context and was a modern aspect of both monarchy and the British state. Although a devout Anglican, Victoria was ready to attend Presbyterian services in Scotland and Lutheran services in Germany, and she saw herself equally as the monarch of all her subjects, whatever their faith. Her Proclamation to the People of India of 1858 repudiated any right or desire to impose on the faith of her subjects and promised all, irrespective of religion, the rights of law. On her state visits to Ireland in 1861 and 1900, Victoria met the heads of the Catholic hierarchy, in

1868 she visited a Catholic mass in Switzerland, and in 1887 Pope Leo XIII was allowed to send an envoy to congratulate Victoria on her Golden Jubilee. The Queen was conspicuously gracious to him. This Queen of all faiths was a long way from Reformation monarchy, or even that which had followed the Glorious Revolution.

The Golden and Diamond jubilees of Victoria, in 1887 and 1897 respectively, showed how much Empire was part of British identity. There was much striking of imperial themes, and much talk of Britain as the uniquely successful imperial power, but, at the same time, the Empire itself was in flux, and, as the old Queen breathed her last in 1901, cracks were appearing in the edifice of Empire. Thanks, in part, to the diffusion within the Empire of British notions of community, identity and political action, and British practices of politicisation, specifically democratisation, which in 1884 brought the right to vote to the majority of adult males in Britain, there was a measure of opposition to imperial control. The Indian National Congress, formed in 1885 and the Egyptian National Party, criticised the nature of imperial control; but there was also a considerable measure of compliance with British rule. In Ireland, the preferred option was 'Home Rule' under the Crown, not republican independence, which was the preference of only a minority. It was far from clear how the British Empire would develop. Different goals and strategies were actively pushed, but, at that point, Dominion status, effective independence under the Crown within an Empire of co-operation, appeared not only an ideal but also a workable proposition.

Imperialism was an aspect of globalisation, and the latter was far more insistent in its impact on British society than Empire itself. If large numbers emigrated to Canada, Australia and New Zealand, more people went to the United States than to any of these imperial possessions, while, in contrast, the number who emigrated to the new and established colonies in Africa and Asia was small. Trade benefited from imperial markets, but non-imperial trading partners, such as Germany, were also important, although tariffs in these cases hit the market for British goods.

Late nineteenth-century problems

Imports from Empire (Australasian wool, mutton and lamb, and Canadian wheat), as well as from outside Empire (American wheat, Argentinian beef, Danish bacon) affected British agriculture greatly in what became the Great Agricultural Depression. Landlords and rural workers found their livelihood affected, as rents and jobs ebbed. The longer-term decline in manufacturing outside the coal-based regions of the Industrial Revolution compounded problems in some rural areas, for example East Anglia.

The late nineteenth-century agrarian crisis helped lead to the decline in the wealth and power of much of the aristocracy, unless they could prop themselves up on mineral rights or marriage with heiresses, notably American, the subject of much speculation in real life and in the plots of novels. This decline was an aspect of a major change on the land, with the old order very much challenged by new money. Such a tension was far from new, but the process was speeded up by agrarian depression and by the extent to which the profits of finance and industry were readily transferable, through estate-purchase, to the creation of a new, affluent, part-time ruralism. This conduct hit notions of landed continuity and rural paternalism. Privilege and the landed élite also served as key targets for political radicals, notably in Ireland and Scotland where rural society was more divided and where Celtic nationalism could play a role.

In contrast to the crisis on the land, the impact of food imports on prices greatly benefited the urban working class, providing the background for political disputes over free trade in the 1900s, 1910s and 1920s. Affluent workers provided a key support for the growth of consumerism which affected both the world of things and leisure activities. Tourism and sport developed as organised capitalist activities, the cinema joined the music hall, while food outlets multiplied, the first permanent Lyons teashop being founded in 1894.

Low pay, casual work and underemployment ensured, however, that many in the working class, both urban and rural, could not share in these benefits. Furthermore, by the close of the century, British industry faced growing international competition. Being the first industrial nation had a major disadvantage as later states could take advantage of newer technology in their first industrial phases. Poverty, however, was not the only prospect for the less affluent. Many emigrated, including from England, and emigration became an important part of Scottish and, even more, Irish identity.

Nationalism

Irish politicians pursued first Catholic Emancipation, with Daniel O'Connell creating a mass democratic movement, and, subsequently, the prospect of 'Home Rule'. Both were major challenges to the practice of British politics, but many British politicians were willing to accommodate these Irish demands.

Scots benefited greatly from the British Empire. The fact that Scotland retained considerable independence within the United Kingdom also militated against political nationalism. It had its own established Church and educational system, as well as a distinctive legal system. Furthermore, in 1885 the Scottish Office and Secretary were created, while five of the ten prime ministers between 1880 and 1935 were Scottish.

Scottishness was an aspect of Britishness, as with the military, politics and trade of Scotland. Scotland was also a local imperial identity, the same fundamentally as being British and Canadian. Britain, indeed, was an imperial state which was multinational in its Britishness. Individual careers reflected the significance of British links. Gladstone, born in England of two Scottish parents, retained a Scottish connection, but Liverpool, Oxford, London and Hawarden were also crucial to his life and experience. He was part of a British élite.

Although with important variations of their own, the Scots subscribed to the prevalent Whig interpretation of history, a public myth that offered a comforting and glorious account that appeared appropriate for a state which ruled much of the globe and which was exporting its constitutional arrangements to other parts of the world. The British viewed convulsions elsewhere, such as the French uprisings in 1830 and 1848, the American Civil War of 1861–5, and the Paris Commune of 1870–1, as evidence of the apparent political failure and backwardness of these states, and of the superiority of Britain. A progressive move towards liberty was discerned in Britain past and present.

For England, this progress was portrayed within a seamless web that stretched back to the supposedly free and democratic village communities of Angles and Saxons applauded by John Richard Green in his *Short History of the English People* (1874). An idealisation of democracy as inherently English was in line with the politics of the spreading franchise. Then, after the setback of the Norman Conquest, the successful quest for liberty could be traced to Magna Carta in 1215, and to other episodes which could be presented as constitutional struggles in medieval England, as well as forwards to the extensions of the franchise in 1832, 1867 and 1884, which were seen as arising naturally from the country's development.

National independence was another theme, with the rejection of foreign control and challenges emphasised, as in the treatment of Henry VIII, the Reformation and Elizabeth I, for example by J. A. Froude in his *History of England from the Fall of Wolsey to the Defeat of the Spanish Armada* (1858–70). The Protestant approach coloured the treatment of post-Roman Britain. For example, the 1815 edition of the *Encyclopaedia Britannica*, a work first published in 1768–71 by a consortium of Edinburgh printers, noted that:

> The reign of Edgar [959–75] proved one of the most fortunate mentioned in the ancient English history. He took the most effectual methods both for preventing tumults at home and invasions from abroad. ... The greatness of King Edgar, which is very much celebrated by the English historians, was owing to the harmony which reigned between him and his subjects; and the reason of this good agreement was that the king sided with Dunstan [Archbishop of Canterbury, 959–88] and the [Benedictine] monks, who had acquired a great ascendant over the people. He enabled them to accomplish their favourite scheme of dispossessing the secular canons of all the monasteries; and he consulted them not only in ecclesiastical but also in civil affairs. On these accounts, he is celebrated by the monkish writers with the highest praises; though it is plain, from some of his actions, that he was a man who could be bound neither by the ties of religion nor humanity.

Britain's empire was given a strong and long historical component, by being presented as apogee and conclusion of a historical process begun with ancient Rome. Architecture reflected this reference to past glory, but also the variety of cultural references deployed in Victorian Britain. The neo-Classicism of the late eighteenth century drew heavily on Roman models, but that of the early nineteenth was dominated by Greek Revival. Neo-Gothic was also highly influential, notably in ecclesiastical architecture. Its case was pushed hard by Augustus Pugin (1812–52), an architect who saw Gothic as the quintessentially Christian style. His arguments and designs hit home at the right moment as, after a long period in which relatively few new churches had been built, there was a period of massive church-building. This owed much to the expansion of the cities and to a determination to resist 'godlessness'. Influential architects in the Gothic Revival included Sir George Gilbert Scott, William Butterfield, G. E. Street, Norman Shaw and Alfred Waterhouse. There was also much secular building in the Gothic style, notably from the 1850s, including the Houses of Parliament by Sir Charles Barry. Pride was readily apparent in new cityscapes. 'Visit to Birkenhead', a piece published in *The Living Age* on 5 July 1845, referred to Merseyside becoming 'the grandest monument which the nineteenth century has erected to the genius of Commerce and Peace'.

The sense of British superiority was also reaffirmed through a combination of the notion of the leader of civilisation with the precepts of Social Darwinism, the idea of an inherent competitiveness leading to a survival of the fittest, which was seen as a way to affirm Britain's success. Charles Darwin himself reflected Britain's role in science and its popularization. His *The Origin of Species by Means of Natural Selection* (1859) was the key work in the field.

Heroic nationalism was a theme across social classes and for all generations. Charles Kingsley (1819–75), a clergyman who was Regius Professor of Modern History at Cambridge from 1860 to 1869, wrote a number of historical novels glorifying heroes from the English past. These included *Westward Ho!* (1855), an account of the Elizabethan struggle with Philip II of Spain, in which the Inquisition and the Jesuits appear as a cruel inspiration of Spanish action, and *Hereward the Wake* (1866) about resistance to the Norman Conquest.

In his popular adventure stories for boys, the war correspondent George Alfred Henty (1832–1902) looked at past as well as present.

His historical accounts, which continued to enjoy substantial sales until after World War Two, included the novels *Under Drake's Flag* (1883), *With Clive in India: or the Beginnings of an Empire* (1884), *St George for England: A Tale of Cressy* [Crécy] *and Poitiers* (1885), *With Wolfe in Canada: The Winning of a Continent* (1887), which stressed Britain's trans-oceanic destiny, and *Held Fast for England: A Tale of the Siege of Gibraltar* (1892), accounts respectively of victories in the sixteenth, eighteenth, fourteenth and eighteenth (twice more) centuries. These books were available in my newly constructed local public library in the 1960s.

There were contrary voices, including those who focused on widespread social hardship, and others who saw Britain's status as under threat from the economic and naval rise of other powers, particularly the USA and Germany. However, at the close of the nineteenth century, there was a stronger sense of national success and pride than there had been at the close of earlier centuries. This pride was expressed at the centre of the imperial capital. Whitehall had grand new ministerial buildings, notably the new War Office (1899–1905) and the new Public Offices (1899–1915). The Mall, the redesigned ceremonial avenue from the refronted Buckingham Palace to Trafalgar Square was finished in 1913 as a memorial to Queen Victoria, whose statue commands the *rond-point* in front of the palace. This suggested a Britain of traditional power far removed from the creation of wealth. So also did Tower Bridge, built in the late 1880s with Neo-Gothic embellishments. Yet, the bridge was right up to date in terms of technology, with stationary steam engines powering hydraulic accumulators to raise the bridge's road platform. At this point, Britain appeared well able to reconcile past and future, history and technology.

CHAPTER FIVE

From 1900 to the present

The outside world dramatically moulded the history of Britain during the twentieth century. This was not only as a result of Britain's central and transformative role in two world wars (1914–18, 1939–45). In addition, the reality and sense of international competition, both political and economic, affected much of the policy of government.

There are long-term trends over which government had only limited control or even influence, including increasing life expectancy, greater urbanisation, and the pace and impact of secularisation; but the impact of international competition was more insistent than these other factors for ministries. Thus, in the early years of the century, social welfare was not the sole reason for legislative change. There was also a sense that modernisation was necessary were Britain to compete in a more challenging world. The serious initial military failures in the Boer War in South Africa (1899–1902) punctured a national confidence already under serious pressure from industrial rivalry with Germany. Modernisation led the Conservatives unsuccessfully to attempt in the 1900s and early 1910s to introduce tariffs, both in order to protect British industry (and jobs) from international competition and to strengthen the economic links of empire. Concerned that tariffs might lead to higher food prices, the electorate rejected the Conservatives.

Instead, it was the Liberal governments in 1905–14 that pushed through major changes. These included the Trade Disputes Act of 1906, which gave trade unions immunity from actions for damages as a result of strike action, and the Parliament Act of 1911 that ended the House of Lords' veto of Commons' legislation. The National Insurance Act of 1911 provided for unemployment assistance. This legislation brought many changes to British politics and society. The establishment of National Insurance meant that every skilled worker now had a number and a numbered card. The classification and analysis of society stemmed from such comprehensive coverage.

The Liberal governments also felt forced to spend large sums on building up the navy in order to stay ahead in a naval race with Germany. Concern about Germany encouraged closer British relations with France from 1904. This led Britain further toward confrontation with Germany.

World War One, 1914–18

Yet, the government was divided in 1914 when war broke out. The German invasion of Belgium, a neutral power guaranteed by Britain, attacked in order to aid the German invasion of France, was crucial to the British decision to fight, as it gave a moral imperative to the outbreak of hostilities. World War One is generally remembered in terms of the trench warfare of the Western Front in France and Belgium where many died without major gains of territory, and the war has been seen as the epitome of military futility. This has tended to lead many commentators, notably at the time of the centenary in 2014, to underrate both the reasons for entry into the war – to prevent German domination of Europe – and also British success in defeating Germany in 1918. This success owed much to the development of effective artillery–infantry co-ordination in launching and sustaining attacks. Furthermore, although the conditions of military service were grim, there was a general sense of resolution, conscientious objectors were not numerous, and many soldiers appear to have relished aspects of military service.

The length and severity of the struggle ensured that the ability to mobilise and apply resources, especially men and munitions, was crucial to the war effort, and also led to an extension of the regulatory powers of the government. The Defence of the Realm Act of 1914 greatly increased the powers of government, which took over control of the railways (1914), the coal mines (1917) and the flour mills (1918). New ministries were created for labour and shipping, a food production department was established in 1917, and food rationing was introduced.

The scale of the war effort was unprecedented. By the end of the war, the Royal Arsenal at Woolwich employed over 80,000 people. Other communities also registered the impact of the war. In London's northern suburbs, Edmonton gained a large military hospital, while Enfield became a major centre for munitions production. Conscription, the absence of which had for long been treated as an aspect of British liberty, was introduced in 1916. This helped to push the size of the armed forces up to 4.5 million in 1917–18, one in three of the male labour force.

Unlike in previous wars, there was no general election during the conflict, and, although created in conditions of political controversy and division, coalition governments provided a high level of political cohesion. This was also to be the pattern in World War Two. Attempts to rally public opinion included the formation of the Department of Information, which, in 1918, became a ministry. Responding to the propaganda possibilities of cinema, the War Office created a Cinematograph Committee.

Surveillance also became more important, with a major growth in numbers and powers. Special Branch numbers rose from 80 in 1914 to 700 in 1918, and MI5 from 14 to 844. Domestic opposition to the war was limited, although, in 1916, a nationalist rebellion in Dublin, the Easter Rising, was launched. It was rapidly suppressed. However, subsequent retribution against nationalist leaders and sympathisers helped rally support to their cause.

More generally, war was a major force for social and political change. Traditional assumptions were questioned and social practices altered. Female employment rose and new roles, many in industry, were played by women, although female wages were lower and, in factories, women were controlled by male foremen.

There was also a major change in the franchise. The Representation of the People Act of 1918 led to universal male suffrage (for those aged 21 or older) as well as a limited degree of women's suffrage: the vote was extended to women of 30 and over, as long as they were householders or the wives of householders. The women most likely to have worked in factories during the war were younger and did not get the vote. Nevertheless, the transition from aristocracy to democracy was now largely complete. In 1928, women gained the vote on the same basis as men, ensuring that in the 1929 election the electorate was 32 million compared to 7.7 million in 1910.

The war also helped the rise of Labour. This was especially so by splitting the Liberal party between the supporters of Herbert Asquith and David Lloyd George, who replaced him as Prime Minister in 1916. This split wrecked the principal political force in pre-war Britain. As Prime Minister, Lloyd George was dependent on Conservative support. Meanwhile, Labour served in the coalition government.

The inter-war years

Although Britain was one of the victors, and its empire therefore expanded considerably in Africa and the Middle East, the war had exhausted the economy, public finances and society. It proved impossible to sustain post-war international ambitions, not least as an immediate economic boom rapidly gave way to a slump, although domestically the war did not lead to the political division seen in Italy, another victor, let alone in defeated Germany.

Instead, in Britain, there was a general feeling that to push matters to extremes would be to betray the many who had died. This attitude helped explain the relative passivity of the short-lived General Strike in 1926. For Stanley Baldwin, Conservative leader in 1923–37 and Prime Minister in 1923–4, 1924–9 and 1935–7, the war reinforced his commitment to service, on a personal level and in terms of the wider nation. The camaraderie of trench life gave Harold Macmillan, Conservative Prime Minister in 1957–63, a determination, when he began his political career, to find a 'middle way' between capitalism and socialism.

The absence of any tradition, since the seventeenth century, of the violent overthrow of authority was also very important, in the response to the post-war Slump, the unsuccessful General Strike, and the large-scale Depression of the 1930s. Nevertheless, labour unrest in England and Scotland after World War One led to concern about political and social stability. This concern produced anxiety about Communist subversion, as well as restrictive legislation such as the Firearms Act of 1920, under which gun ownership was dependent on licences issued by the police and renewed annually. This was very different to the position in the USA.

In Ireland, the situation contrasted with that in England and Scotland. The nationalist party, Sinn Féin, won the majority of Irish seats in the 1918 general election. The Union with Ireland had been greatly weakened by the failure to respond adequately to the Home Rule movement and by the willingness prior to the war to countenance Unionist resistance to it. The response to the Easter Rising was also a significant factor in helping Sinn Féin win support.

The government initially resisted Irish nationalism. However, in 1920–1, in reaction to guerrilla warfare and terrorism by the Irish Republic Army, the government gave way. Nationalist acceptance of partition was the price for the government eventually agreeing a settlement. The nationalists gained control of what became the Irish Free State, the bulk of the island. As a distinct new territory, the Protestant-dominated Northern Ireland (most, but not all, of the historic province of Ulster) remained part of the United Kingdom, which became the United Kingdom of Great Britain and Northern Ireland.

Elsewhere, Britain faced serious opposition in some other parts of the empire, notably Iraq, India and Egypt, as well as in areas of new commitments outside the empire, notably Turkey. Although the government backed down in the last case in 1922, opposition in Iraq, India and Egypt was overcome.

There was no comparable disruption in Britain. In England, Scotland and Wales, had the General Strike of 1926 led to widespread violence or to a change of government, neither of which was the intention of the trade union leadership or membership, then the political situation in the 1930s during the Depression might have been less propitious. However, although the background was of a rapidly changing country, the combination of this change with an inherent political stability was notable.

Place and movement were particularly changeable, as urban Britain altered and the motor car spread in a symbiotic development: cars encouraged housing of a lower density. The tightly packed terraces characteristic of the Victorian city, for the middle as well as the working class, were supplemented by miles of 'semis': semi-detached houses with mock-Tudor elevations, red-tiled roofs, and walls of red brick or pebble-dash, with a small front and larger back garden, each with a small drive and a garage. These houses were built in large numbers, not only around London, but also on routes leaving all major towns, especially in areas of prosperity, such as much of southern England.

Suburbia had spread in the late nineteenth century with the railways, but development then had generally not moved far from the stations. In contrast, car transport permitted less intensive development. In advertisements, cars were pictured against backdrops of mock-Tudor suburban houses. Building on new sites away from city centres ensured that cheap land was used. This usage helped reduce the cost of housing, but new houses ate up land. The majority of new homes were for owner-occupiers who commuted to work by car or train, including via the electrified lines south of London and the spreading Underground routes to the north of the city.

The semis were to be criticised as lacking in individuality, being wasteful of space, and being dependent on the car. However, the sameness of suburbia was deliberate: a predictability of product helped make new houses sell, while the houses were mass-produced and had standardised components. This reflected the dominance of brick as a building material and the use of prefabricated doors and windows. In the mid-1920s, new houses cost between £400 and £1,000. The ability to borrow at low rates of interest from building societies in order to buy houses on mortgages was important to the housing market. The new transport system helped lessen costs because lorries could move housing materials from central manufacturing sites, including large brickworks, as at Peterborough, and factories making prefabricated doors and windows.

As with the car, the semi expressed freedom, a freedom to escape the constraints of living in close proximity to others and, instead, to enjoy space. Semis were not the suburban villas of the wealthier members of the middle class, but they captured the aspirations of millions, and offered them a decent living environment. Unlike my father, who grew up in the crowded East End of London, but, thanks to him, I was able to enjoy the space of a semi. There was also the building of much public housing, in part as a result of slum clearing. Many, however, continued to face harsh conditions in deprived areas.

In the interwar period (1918–39), private ownership of cars increased more than tenfold, to reach nearly two million by September 1938. Car production rose from 116,000 in 1924 to

341,000 in 1938. Moreover, having made little progress in road building during the earlier century of rail, Britain now embarked upon a massive programme of constructing and upgrading existing roads in order to provide all-weather surfaces for cars. The Trunk Roads Programme, largely paid for by central government, was devised in 1929, both to provide employment and to ensure that road improvement schemes were pressed forward.

Cars and roads led to new smells, as well as 'the sound of horns and motors' of T. S. Eliot's poem *The Waste Land* (1922). The visual context of life was affected, with signs, lampposts and traffic lights. Roads led to new boundaries and commands, to zebra crossings, and to the flashing safety lamps called Belisha beacons, named after a Minister of Transport, Leslie Hore-Belisha. Large numbers of drivers and others, however, were killed in road accidents, with 7,000 deaths annually for a number of years in the 1930s. The police found that enforcing the traffic laws became a major commitment. Whereas about 2 per cent of committals were to do with transport in 1900, more than 52 per cent of committals were connected with road offences by the early 1930s. As a result, the middle class were brought into contact with the law to an unprecedented extent.

Now, we are well aware of the damage and disruption brought by road transport, not least the resulting pollution. However, for much of the twentieth century, the freedom offered made cars seductive. In the interwar years, those who could not afford cars were in the overwhelming majority, but vehicle ownership became a goal or model for many, creating a pent-up aspiration, and ensuring that future affluence would lead to the purchase of more cars.

The cinema helped to foster this romance: films, both British and their influential American counterparts, created and disseminated lifestyles and images. Going to the cinema was a common activity and gave a communal feel to what would later, with television and, even more, the internet, become more individual. By 1939, Birmingham alone had 110 cinemas. Cars were not alone. There were 53,000 buses and coaches by September 1938 and their availability also changed the experience of travel.

The growing motor car industry, centred on new sites such as the Morris works at Cowley, Oxford, was an aspect of the expansion of high-productivity consumer manufacturing, rather than traditional export industries, such as shipbuilding and cotton-textiles. This expansion contributed to the growth rate in gross national product per head, which was about 1.5 per cent in the 1920s compared to 0.4 per cent in 1900–13.

Nevertheless, there was also considerable poverty and unemployment. The geography of economic opportunity was reflected in the response to the General Strike of 1926 which arose from the crisis in labour relations in the coal industry where falling exports led to pressure to cut wages. The strike was solidly supported in London, most coalfield towns and some other cities, including Birmingham and Liverpool, but support was far weaker across much of southern England. Government firmness, including the willingness to deploy troops, led the Trade Union Congress to call off the strike.

Labour governments took office in 1924 and 1929, but they were minority administrations dependent on Liberal support. Throughout the decade, the Conservatives were the party with the largest percentage of the popular vote, while, until 1929, they also had most seats in Parliament. The conservatism of the 1920s, particularly among the newly enfranchised female electorate, was also revealed in local elections. This conservatism represented a continuation of the consolidation of the propertied that had begun in the 1880s as growing Liberal radicalism led to middle-class disaffection and a rallying to the Conservatives.

Established in 1929, Ramsay MacDonald's Labour government faced the major challenge of the Great Depression of the 1930s, which began with the Slump of 1929. World trade fell, greatly harming Britain, a major exporter, and accentuating already-apparent weaknesses in the factors that had earlier led to industrial growth. These problems led to a marked rise in the number of unemployed: from 1.6 million in 1929 to 3.4 million, about 17 per cent of the labour force, in 1932. The government, unable both to sustain public expenditure, and thus preserve social welfare levels, notably in unemployment pay, and to defend the pound, was bitterly divided and resigned in 1931.

The Labour government was replaced by a National Government, again, under MacDonald, but largely composed of Conservatives, and opposed by the bulk of the Labour Party. This government, the establishment of which had been encouraged by King George V (r. 1910–36), appeared necessary to keep a national emergency at bay. It won overwhelming victories in the general elections of 1931 and 1935, the second the only election in the century in which the government won a majority of the popular vote. The National Government acted as a force for stability and helped ensure that Britain avoided the political extremism seen across most of Europe. Moreover, alongside the serious hardships of the 1930s, with 2.2 million people still unemployed in 1938, there was also much prosperity. Gross National Product (GNP) returned to its 1929 figure in 1934, the economy recovered more than those of France and the USA, about 2.6 million jobs were created in 1933–8, real wages rose, and prices fell. UK Gross Domestic Product (GDP) rose at an average of 2.2 per cent per year from 1924 to 1937, an account that does not match the recovered memory on offer for the 1930s.

There were, indeed, major contrasts between the situation in prosperous areas, such as London, and those that were depressed, particularly mining and heavy industrial areas, notably in South Wales, North-East England and industrial Scotland. All of these areas saw misery as well as the emigration of part of their workforce. This experience of the Depression was to be significant for the post-1945 Labour government.

Yet, it is easy to see why, but for World War Two, there probably would not have been a Labour government after the next election, which was due in 1940. Aside from the boom in housing, which led to three million new homes being built in the 1930s, including large numbers of council houses, there were growing industries then that were focused on consumer demand.

This demand was linked to a marked shift in the world of things. A National Grid for electricity, developed under the control of the Central Electricity Board, had been established under the Electricity Supply Act of 1926, and household electricity supplies expanded greatly, replacing coal, gas, candles and human effort. Electricity was seen as clean and convenient, and as a way to improve the environment, and power, heat and light were increasingly dependent on electricity. Refrigeration had a major impact on food storage and thus on the range of food available in households with fridges. In his 1938 detective novel *Invisible Weapons*, John Rhode captured change in a British cottage: 'Everything here's absolutely up to date ... all the latest gadgets – tiled bathroom, latest type of gas cooker, electric refrigerator, coke boiler for constant hot water

... a labour-saving house'. The housing boom meant that there were many houses that had to be equipped, and the percentage of homes wired for electricity rose from 31.8 in 1932 to 65.4 in 1938. This had an impact on the consumption of power and the sales of electric cookers, irons, fridges, water heaters and vacuum cleaners. This demand helped industrial expansion.

Such expenditure also reflected, and helped to define, class differences, a key element both in the world of work and in that of things. Whereas radios, vacuum cleaners and electric irons were widely owned, in part thanks to the spread of hire purchase, in contrast, electric fridges, cookers and washing machines were largely restricted to the middle class. These differences were linked to an aspect of the major social divide between those who employed others (increasingly, however, an occasional daily help rather than the less-numerous full-time domestic servants), and the employed. World War One had led to a major fall in the number of servants: from nearly 2.5 million in 1910 to nearly 1.5 million in 1920.

The poor were unable to participate fully in the new leisure society. Most lacked radios and could not afford the cinema, let alone holidays in the new Butlins holiday camps. Such lives were presented in 'Condition of Britain' works, such as George Orwell's *Down and Out in Paris and London* (1933) and *The Road to Wigan Pier* (1937), as well as Walter Greenwood's depiction of the harshness of unemployment in *Love on the Dole* (1933), Walter Brierley's similar *Means Test Man* (1935), and George Blake's Clydeside equivalent *The Shipbuilders* (1935).

Moreover, most of the culture of the period was not designed to challenge established practices and the social order. In a time of upheaval, there was an emphasis on continuity, as in the subordination of women. Dorothy L. Sayers' Harriet Vane was an independent-minded female character who had a lover before she married. However, she was one among a host of female characters who reinforced stable sexual and class identities, such as Agatha Christie's Jane Marple, and the heroines created by Ivy Compton-Burnett and Daphne Du Maurier.

In a similar fashion, the Modernism of writers such as Virginia Woolf had only a limited appeal compared to many of the 'middle'- and 'low'-brow writers of the period. However, Modernism had little airing on the radio broadcasts of the British Broadcasting

Corporation (BBC), established in 1926 as a monopoly acting in the 'national interest'. Indeed, the BBC helped give radio a national character. 'BBC English', the 'Received Pronunciation', set a standard for conformity. Similarly, in music the pastoral work of Ralph Vaughan Williams and the elegiac tones of Edward Elgar remained popular in programmes, gramophone record sales and the radio. The world's first public television broadcasting service began from the BBC in 1936.

More generally, films and newsreels offered an optimistic emphasis on social cohesion and patriotism. Alongside the counter-cultural sexual and alcoholic excess depicted in Evelyn Waugh's novel *Vile Bodies* (1930), D. C. Thomson and Mills and Boon, two of the most successful publishers of popular fiction, actively disseminated conservative social and moral standards: sexual energy was contained, while radicalism, social strain and moral questioning were ignored. Censorship of the stage by the Lord Chamberlain's department continued. This censorship served to maintain moral conventions on topics such as sexuality, abortion and birth control, and thus the role of the past and its codes. Interracial sexuality was particularly deplored, as was the depiction of God.

This conservatism was an expression of a strong view of national identity as inherently conservative and opposed to novelty and radicalism, and was the cultural counterpart of the political position of Stanley Baldwin, the Conservative leader. He replaced MacDonald as Prime Minister in 1935, holding the post until 1937. In opposition to the Communists, as well as to Oswald Mosley's far-right British Union of Fascists, which he presented as un-British, Baldwin stressed national identity, continuity, distinctiveness and stolid common sense. Baldwin did so not in order to embrace political reaction, but rather to seek an imaginative way to lessen tensions arising from economic change, particularly rivalry between capital and labour. Baldwin was photographed with pigs and five-bar gates, helping underline an identification with an image of rural values. This approach proved particularly successful in England, but the Conservatives failed to make a strong impact in Wales.

World War Two, 1939–45

In comparison with the weaknesses and collapse of democracy over much of continental Europe in the 1930s, the success of the National Government was a triumph, and one that was important to national survival in World War Two. This was very much an unwanted war that arose from German, Italian and Japanese aggression. Mistakenly assuming that it would be possible to negotiate with Adolf Hitler, Germany's Nazi dictator, Baldwin's successor, Neville Chamberlain, Prime Minister from 1937 to 1940, sought a negotiated settlement to European differences, notably with the Munich agreement over Czechoslovakia in 1938. This quest was referred to as Appeasement and was to be castigated later as immoral as well as unsuccessful.

At the time, however, the avoidance of war appeared a necessity and Chamberlain was very popular. He had a longstanding concern with cutting expenditure and maintaining financial stability. In 1933, in response to military pressure for greater defence preparations in the Far East, Chamberlain, as Chancellor of the Exchequer, responded, 'at the Treasury, it was felt that the risks of the financial situation were perhaps more pressing than the risks from Japanese aggression'.

In 1939, Hitler's policies shattered the policy of Appeasement, just as Japan was to do in December 1941. The rump of Czechoslovakia was occupied in March 1939. In response to Hitler's breaking of the Munich agreement, Chamberlain sought to deter him by guaranteeing Poland and Romania. Indeed, Britain went to war in September 1939 in response to the German invasion of Poland.

Initially the war went badly. Nothing could be done to help Poland. Moreover, British forces were defeated in 1940 as they unsuccessfully sought to prevent the German conquests of Norway and France. This was a key moment of national defeat and, indeed, of vulnerability in the face of a threatened German invasion. However, this weakness led not to the acceptance of German peace terms as might have been expected in the aftermath of defeat, but to a determination, voiced resolutely, and sustained by Chamberlain's successor, Winston Churchill, to fight on.

German air attacks intended to prepare the way for invasion were blunted, in the Battle of Britain in August and September

1940, by high fighting quality, able command decisions, good fighter aeroplanes, and British radar. British cities, particularly London, were then bombed heavily in the Blitz. The experience of 1940 helped fashion a renewed patriotism. It proved easier to support the war when Britain was unencumbered by allies, albeit receiving the powerful support of the worldwide Empire. German air attacks also appeared to demonstrate the morality of the struggle, as well as encouraging the sense that everyone, irrespective of their background, was under attack. This proved a crucially important memory, both during and after the war.

The British gained allies in 1941 when Germany attacked the Soviet Union (June) and declared war on the USA (December) after Germany's ally, Japan, had launched an assault on both Britain and the USA. Ultimately, this widening of the war was to be decisive in Allied victory, but, in 1941 and early 1942, Germany and Japan made major inroads. The surrender of Singapore in February 1942, after an ignominious campaign in which the British were driven from Malaya, shattered British prestige in Asia. Burma (Myanmar) was lost to Japanese attack soon after.

German and Japanese offensives, however, were blunted in late 1942, the British playing a role by pushing back the Germans from Egypt and keeping the Japanese out of India. The Allies moved over to the offensive. The Battle of the Atlantic against German submarines was won in early 1943, and the Germans were cleared from North Africa as well. Sicily was then invaded in July 1943, mainland Italy that September, and Normandy in June 1944. In Burma, the Japanese were outfought on the ground in 1944–5. British troops fought there alongside Australian, Caribbean, Ceylonese (Sri Lankan), Egyptian, Indian, Kenyan, West African and New Zealand troops, all under British command, a major demonstration of the continued military potency of Empire. Germany and Japan were both defeated in 1945. If the Soviets played the key role on land against the Germans, the British had played an important part against Germany, particularly at sea and in the air.

The impact of the war on Britain itself was gruelling. Although less devastating than had been expected, physical damage was greater than in any previous conflict. Over 60,000 civilians were killed in air and missile attack, nearly half of them in London, much of which was devastated. The damage to the built environment was accentuated by postwar reconstruction, much of which was poor quality. In response to the threat of bombing, there were mass evacuations of children from the major cities, including 690,000 alone from London, the biggest state-directed move of civilians in British history. Disruption greatly hit family life and affected social behaviour. However, despite problems, including the black market, as well as strikes, there was a high degree of acceptance of the need for sacrifice, and morale and popular resolution were higher than has sometimes been suggested.

War also savaged the economy. Export markets were lost, and financial stability was hit by massive expenditure. Britain lost about a quarter of its national wealth during the war, and dependence upon wartime loans (mainly from the USA) made it the world's leading debtor nation in 1945. The debt had serious consequences for post-war Britain.

During the war, government regulation became ubiquitous and new ministries were created in 1939 for economic warfare, food, home security, information, shipping and supply. Later additions included aircraft production, fuel and power, and production. Conscription of men began in 1939 and of women in 1942. Everything was brought under the scrutiny of government. For example, food rationing, introduced in 1940, was not popular, but it remoulded the nation's diet in accordance with nutritional science. The ration card extended the scope of the state and regimented society. At the same time, the rapid growth of the black market reflected a widespread determination to evade the system. The hospital sector was reorganised under the Emergency Medical Service.

War controls made Socialism appear increasingly normal to many; as taxation rose, the scale of government dramatically expanded, belief in planning increased, the cost of living was subsidised, and attitudes towards what was quintessentially British changed. The Labour Party's role in the wartime coalition government formed in 1940 was important to its revived standing, and the war ended with an election victory for Labour, its first clear parliamentary majority, and one that reflected the widespread popularity of its position and programme, as well as a rejection of the Conservatives as the party of the 1930s, now seen in terms of the Depression and of inequality.

What else the post-war world would bring was less clear. In April 1944, the Admiralty discussed plans for a big heavy cruiser, new battleships and carriers following in May. Post-war politics and realities, however, were to lead to very different priorities.

British society since 1945

Britain and the British have both changed profoundly since 1945, and these changes had a greater impact than the doings of politicians which generally dominate accounts. A principal driver in the change in the country has been a major and unprecedented growth in population. This growth has been matched by rapidly rising expectations about lifestyle, as affluence became normative and individuals expressed themselves through creating their own material words. These worlds were, at once, individualistic and also, as a result of pressures from advertising and pricing, conformist.

In the shape of demands for mobility (cars) and space (houses), this growth in population has ensured the transfer of land from agriculture and the wild to roads and housing, with multiple consequences for wildlife and for the human experience of the countryside. Where the latter is not the base for commuting or retirement communities, it has become depopulated as agricultural employment has dramatically declined, in part due to mechanisation. Government action affecting rural life, with scant concern for rural opinion, was seen in 2004 when the long-established practice of fox hunting was banned.

Environmental pressure has been a key element in Britain's development, with demand, for example, for water reflecting not only rising population but also greater comfort and wealth in the shape of more frequent baths or showers, and a greater ownership of dishwashers. This change reflected the strength of consumerism, which focused on mobility, leisure, comfort and the automatic availability of the heat, water and food that previous generations had found it difficult to provide. Home ownership was also a key element: whereas, in 1914, 10 per cent of the English housing stock was owner-occupied, by 2000 the percentage, and of a far larger stock, was 70. In Scotland, where wage levels are lower and the control by local authorities stronger, the percentage is lower.

Animal life has been badly hit by environmental pressure stemming from population increase and consumerism. As an instance, the number of grey partridge fell by about 80 per cent between 1976 and 1998, due in large part to the destruction of nesting sites when hedgerows were grubbed up. On the whole, lowland species were more seriously affected than their upland counterparts by housing developments and agricultural changes. Such changes did not simply affect the wildlife that also live in the country but also made rarer many sights and sounds that had once characterized the country. The diminution (and even disappearance) of the dawn chorus in several parts of the country, and the decline in the number of butterfly species, was a particularly poignant indicator of loss to changes in land use, as well as pollution and pesticides.

As with much else, there is a regional dimension. Thus, the 2007–11 survey by the British Trust for Ornithology indicated an increase in overall populations of woodland, farmland and migrant perching birds in northern England and Scotland, and a decline in the more populous South. Climate change was partly responsible, but development pressures in the South were significant.

Environmental pressures took many forms. Rising sea and river levels linked to global warming were in part responsible for flooding in early 2014 and to a situation then in which the Environment Agency estimated that 5.2 million homes were at risk from flooding. Another long-term issue arose from the pressures and problems created by far larger quantities of rubbish. This rubbish was a consequence of the rise of consumerism, as well as of population numbers.

Environmental crises were related to the issues involved in managing agriculture and the food supply. The BSE (bovine spongiform encephalopathy) scandal affected British beef. The 2001 outbreak of foot-and-mouth disease arose from the mishandling of contaminated waste by a pig farm and led to Britain banning feeding kitchen waste to animals. During the crisis, a ban on the movement of livestock was imposed by the government, public footpaths were closed to prevent the spread of the virus, the European Union banned the export from Britain of animals and meat products, and there was a mass cull of at least four million animals. Smouldering pyres of carcasses became a common sight. The disease was wiped out, but the crisis was traumatic for much of rural Britain.

The vulnerability of the human food-system was shown again with the rise of bovine tuberculosis which led to an increase in the number of cattle slaughtered in England and Wales to over 38,000 in 2012. There was great controversy over whether this disease should be countered by the culling of badgers, controversy which again showed how far farmers were regulated by national agencies.

The change in human numbers has also been linked to a marked transformation in the composition of the population. Due primarily to advances in medicine, and as part of a general trend around the developed world, life expectancy has risen greatly for both men and women; although death rates from coronary heart disease are among the highest in the world. The rise in life expectancy has ensured that the average age of the population has risen, a process accentuated by the extent to which the birth rate has not comparably increased, although there was a baby boom after World War Two. This rising life expectancy has affected the pattern of society and the content of politics, notably with the emphasis placed in the 2010s on supporting the interests of pensioners.

Furthermore, large-scale immigration, particularly from the West Indies and South Asia, but also from other areas, notably in the 2000s Eastern Europe, altered the population, especially in the major cities, although far less so in Scotland. The population as a whole became ethnically far more diverse, with important cultural consequences. In accordance with the British Nationality Act of 1948, which confirmed the existing position in guaranting freedom of entry from the Commonwealth and colonies, there was large-scale immigration from the West Indies and South Asia. Whereas in 1970 there were about 375,000 Hindus, Muslims and Sikhs combined, by 1993 the figure was about 1,620,000, with the rise in the number of Muslims being particularly pronounced.

Social and cultural change have also reflected the extent to which the population has become more individualistic and less deferential. The moral code that prevailed in 1945 was overthrown, a process that began in the 1950s and that was reflected in far-reaching legal changes in the 1960s. Abortion and homosexuality became legal, capital punishment was abolished, and measures were taken to improve the legal position of women. In 1991, the offence of rape was extended to victimhood within marriage.

Alongside such changes came those of women in the world of work. Records on the proportion of women in work began in 1971, an aspect of increased interest in the subject. The percentage was then 52.7 whereas by December 2013 it had risen to 67.2.

Male employment remained higher, at a percentage of 77. Broad and long-term social changes interacted with the impact of more specific policy decisions. The attempts to equalise the pension age of men and women, and to change single-parent benefits, were both significant. The female state pension age is due to rise from 60 to 65 by 2018 and to 66 between 2018 and 2020. This helped lead to a major increase in employment among women over 50. There was still, however, a significant pay gap. In December 2013, this was 15.7 per cent on average.

In addition to changing, or more assertive, gender and youth expectations and roles, there were other broad currents that helped to give a character to the age. The decline of formality in all its respects was a major one. Informality in means of address and conversation became far more pronounced, as did informality in dress which was an aspect of the expression of personality through spending.

Changes in manners and behaviour were also linked to those in social structure and in sexual practice. Divorce rose markedly from the end of World War Two, with a major spike in England and Wales in 1949 followed by a fall in the divorce rate in the 1950s, albeit to a rate considerably above the pre-war rate. In the 1960s, the rate began to rise again, a process eased by the Divorce Reform Act in 1971. From 74,437 divorces in England and Wales in 1971, the figures rose to a record high of 165,018 in 1993, before falling to 147,735 in 2002 and 118,140 in 2012. These figures concealed significant variations notably the growing trend for divorce later in life, which reflected rising expectations, as well as new technology in the shape of links through social media and dating websites and the availability of viagra. Due in large part to divorce, the percentage of single-parent, female-headed households increased, not least from 8.3 per cent of households with children in 1971 to 12.1 per cent in 1980.

This was linked with the widespread end in the relationship between sex and marriage. The NHS (Family Planning) Act passed in 1967 made no mention of marriage. In 2014, Lord Wilson of Culworth, a judge, declared that the traditional nuclear family had been replaced with the 'blended family', with divorce ensuring many 'step-families of the half-blood'.

These changes were linked to shifts in religious practice. By the 1990s, only one in seven Britons was an active member of a

Christian Church, although more claimed to be believers. Both for most believers as well as for the less or non-religious, faith became less important, not only to the fabric of life but also to many of the turning points of individual lives, especially dying and death. This was part of a longer-term trend towards the ascendancy of secular values. The century saw a general and protracted decline in attendance at Easter by Church of England congregations. In 1911, there were 2.3 million Easter Day communicants and over 23,000 clergy. By 1931, there were still 2.3 million communicants and 21,309 clergy, albeit for a larger population. By 1951, these figures had fallen to 1.9 million and 18,196 and by 1966 to 1.8 million and 20,008 clergy. The estimated Roman Catholic population increased markedly over the same period: from 1.7 million in 1911 (of whom 915,000 actually attended Mass), to 3.55 million (2.1 million Mass attendance) in 1961, 4.1 million in 1969 and over 5 million by 1976. However, when taken as a proportion of the total population, the overall percentage attending Church remained relatively small.

The failure in the 1990s of the 'Keep Sunday Special' campaign, heavily backed by the Established Churches, to prevent shops from opening on the Sabbath, confirmed the general trend. Churches had played a major role in charitable functions and the provision of social welfare, but these were largely replaced by the state, albeit with many gaps.

The lives of most politicians ceased to be illuminated by religious values. Whereas developments in the faith of, for example, Gladstone or Baldwin had been important, that was less the case with Wilson or Heath. National days of prayer, announced with the approval of the government and expected to engage the general population rather than simply Church congregations, ended in 1947, when one was held in response to severe economic difficulties. The Cabinet considered another in 1957, but rejected the idea. This end reflected not just a change in the political atmosphere but also on the part of Church leaders now accepting the role of secularisation.

More generally, the authority of age and experience were overthrown and, in their place, came an emphasis on youth and novelty. This was seen in politics with, for example, the lowering of the voting age to 18, and discussion, in the 2010s, about a lowering to 16, the age used for the Scottish referendum in 2014.

An emphasis on youth and novelty was also seen in the economy, with the rise of the youth consumer; and in culture, with marked changes in popular music. The 1960s more generally destroyed a cultural continuity that had lasted from the Victorian period. This destruction reflected the impact of social and ideological trends, not least shifts in the understanding of gender, youth, class, place and race. These trends also affected the built environment, with much torn down in the 1960s. A well-meaning but often misguided, and sometimes corrupt, combination of developers, planners and city councils, convinced that the past should be discarded, embarked on widespread devastation and trashy rebuilding in cities such as Leeds, Manchester, Newcastle and Exeter.

Another instance of the lack of interest in the past was seen with the treatment of key historic sites. The car, in the shape of the A303 and the A308, dominates Stonehenge and Runnymede (where Magna Carta was agreed) respectively, as well as battlefields such as Naseby.

Alongside the apparent continuity in popular culture of works such as the James Bond films, the novels of Dick Francis and the radio soap *The Archers*, there were also important shifts, for example in popular music. In the 1960s, the latter, not least the songs sung by the Beatles (whose debut single 'Love Me Do' was released in October 1962) and the Rolling Stones, gave Britain a very different feel in the world to that it had had as the world's leading empire. The promotion of pop music through the establishment of Radio One and the role of pirate radio stations drove change home. Particularly in the shape of the Beatles, who came from Merseyside, pop music challenged the 'Received Pronunciation' of the language, offering a regional difference that was taken up by the BBC where the importance of conformity in diction, style and tone declined from the 1960s. Colour television from 1967 dramatised a sense of change: everything before now seemed grey.

Legislation also played a role in the engagement with change. Social legislation was significant, much introduced by the 1964–70 Labour governments. 'The New Britain' was the title of Labour's 1964 manifesto. Indeed, 1960s' 'liberation' is generally thought of in terms of youth, sex and social liberalism.

Legislation that led to the expansion of consumerism was also important. Consumerism was related to a range of factors in the broader culture of the period, including the dominance of the individual and individual preferences in social mores and practices, the ethos of the house owner, and the decline of 'elitist' public-spirited notions of culture in favour of those focused on user preferences. To critics, there was a disengagement with social concerns as part of a breakdown of civil society.

Consumerism changed and developed as a result of the abolition of Resale Price Maintenance (RPM) by the Conservative government in 1964. RPM had obliged shops to sell goods at standard prices set by suppliers, and thus prevented the search for more business through undercutting. This helped small independent shopkeepers in their resistance to multiples. Once RPM was abolished, it became easier for supermarkets, benefiting from economies of scale, such as mass purchasing, to offer pricing structures that drove competitors out of business. Consumer preference for supermarkets led to a marked degree of sameness in shopping, which was accentuated as products that they had not previously sold, such as alcohol and petrol, became available. Supermarkets proved the prime site for activity in the age of affluence created by the per capita rise in GDP by 40 per cent between 1950 and 1966.

The end of empire

The Liverpool Sound, the Swinging Sixties, and the London of Carnaby Street and the mini-skirt, created an image far removed from that of 1956 when, in a last major flourish of imperial power, Britain, in the Suez Crisis, had unsuccessfully sought to intimidate Egypt. In 1945, Britain still had the largest empire in the world, and in 1946 Admiral Willis, Commander-in-Chief Mediterranean, could write about his optimism for a long-term, albeit smaller-scale, presence in Egypt. That, however, was to go the way of the big-gun navy. Britain's last battleship was scrapped in 1960.

Beginning with independence for India and Pakistan in 1947, the Empire was largely granted independence by 1964, particularly the African colonies, although imperial fragments remained. The process of imperial departure was especially rapid in 1957–64. Earlier, it had been assumed that Empire could continue after Indian independence, and there was a determined effort in the early 1950s to keep both idea and practice alive; but governmental attitudes changed significantly after Suez. The following year, in 1957, in his novel *Landed Gently*, Alan Hunter referred to jingoism as doomed alongside other aspects of the old world, notably the satanic mills and social injustice.

Withdrawal from Europe was not only a British phenomenon, France granting most of its African colonies independence in 1960. The most populous fragment of Empire, Hong Kong, was handed over to China in 1997, but a war was successfully fought with Argentina in 1982 when the latter attacked the Falkland Islands, a colony since 1833, inhabited by British settlers.

As Empire had played a major role in British senses of identity, its loss was an important discontinuity, although younger generations did not feel this. Indeed, this constituted an important contrast in the historical memory and imagination between generations. An attempt was made to offer a different identity in the shape of the Commonwealth, which was seen as a way to retain imperial cohesion and strength, but it succumbed to the reality of different interests and concerns. Few beside Elizabeth II (r. 1952–) took much interest in the Commonwealth.

As Empire receded fast, Britain seemed a diminished power, although it had an enhanced military capability as a result of becoming the third state in the world to gain the atom bomb (1952), followed by the hydrogen bomb (1957). Defence focused on the protection of Western Europe against the threat of Soviet invasion, and Britain played a key role in this confrontation, which was known as the Cold War. An active member of international organisations, not least with a permanent seat on the United Nations Security Council, of which it was a founder member, Britain was also a founder member of NATO (the North Atlantic Treaty Organisation) in 1949, and sent a contingent of troops to take part in the United Nations forces engaged in the Korean War (1950–3) against Communist North Korea. Having withdrawn its garrisons and bases from east of Suez in the 1960s and early 1970s, British forces returned there from the 1990s, albeit as part of American-led coalitions.

Politics and economics in Britain

Closer to home, troops were deployed in Northern Ireland from 1969 in response to an outbreak in sectarian violence which rapidly became a major terrorist challenge. The Catholic nationalist Provisional IRA proved a durable terrorist organisation. A peaceful end to the 'Troubles' there was negotiated, with the Good Friday Agreement in 1998, but tension continues.

In contrast, Welsh and Scottish nationalism remained essentially peaceful, and in 1999 each gained a devolved assembly exercising a considerable amount of control. At times, Britain itself appeared to be going the same way as a devolved entity within Europe, because entry into the EEC (European Economic Community), later EU (European Union), in 1973 led to a marked erosion of national sovereignty and to a transfer of powers to European institutions. Paradoxically, fiscal weakness in 1992, when Britain had to leave the European Exchange Rate Mechanism, helped maintain a degree of national autonomy. This continued when Britain stayed outside the euro.

At the national level, government was controlled by the Labour Party (1945–51, 1964–70, 1974–9, 1997–2010), and its Conservative rival (1951–64, 1970–4, 1979–97), and, until 2010, there were no coalition ministries, unlike for much of the period from 1915 to 1945. There were major areas of overlap between the two parties, particularly when they were in office, for example in maintaining free healthcare at the point of delivery, the basis of the National Health Service, and also in a measure of corporatism until the 1980s. There were also major contrasts, notably in 1979–90, when the Conservative Margaret Thatcher was the country's first female Prime Minister and corporatism was largely abandoned.

Even from 1945 to 1975, when Thatcher became Party leader, replacing the more corporatist Edward Heath, the Conservatives tended to favour individual liberty and low taxation, while Labour preferred collectivist solutions and were therefore happier to advocate a leading, controlling role for the state. This was seen in particular with Labour support for the nationalisation of major parts of the economy during their 1945–51, 1964–70 and 1974–9 governments. The nationalisations helped to cripple Britain's recovery from damage done by World War Two.

Most parts, in turn, were denationalised under the Conservatives in 1979–97, a policy that combined ideology in the shape of rolling back the state with economic policy. They were not subsequently nationalised under Labour, which held power from 1997 to 2010.

Under Labour, there were calls for a transformation in society, and notably so in the 1970s and 1980s, as the party moved away from a social democratic path comparable to its Continental counterparts. In the manifesto for the general election of February 1974, there was a 'proud' declaration of 'Socialist aims' and a commitment to 'a fundamental and irreversible shift in the balance of power and wealth in favour of working people and their families'. As the party became closer to radical trade unions, so the emphasis shifted from the classless rhetoric of the mid-1960s to a stress on the workers.

This emphasis helped accentuate a sense of political division, both under the weak Labour governments of 1974–9 and then under their Conservative successors of 1979–97. Bitter divisions between parties were matched by those within them, and the overall impression in the 1970s in particular was of a nation in collapse. Social and industrial cohesion appeared threatened, and there was widespread concern about rising crime levels. There was a widespread anxiety that Britain was broken and finished, and this anxiety encouraged lurid talk in the 1970s of the need for extra-parliamentary solutions.

In the end, the political system held, social peace was maintained, and Margaret Thatcher came to power through a general election. She then used successive electoral mandates to push through major changes. In the process, Thatcher shattered much of the 'moral economy' of post-war corporatist society, notably in its 1970s' form, and challenged a range of interests, from trade unions to the traditional structure of the City of London. Thatcher was able to do so in part because this 'moral economy' had already faced a crisis in the divided 1970s, a decade in which confidence in established practices declined. Thatcher also benefited greatly in her 1983 and 1987 electoral victories from the split in the opposition between a weak Labour Party and the new Social Democratic Party which, largely composed of dissidents from Labour's extremism, aligned with, and eventually merged with, the Liberal Party.

In pushing through her agenda, Thatcher overcame attempts, both by the radical leadership of the miners' union and by

Irish terrorists, to overthrow the political process. At the same time, Thatcher's policies helped to change the social politics and environment of many communities across Britain. The collapse of the coal industry reflected international economic trends, but her deliberate marginalisation of the industry left many former pit communities bereft.

Tony Blair, Labour Party leader from 1994 to 2007 and the Prime Minister from 1997 to 2007, sought to temper traditional Labour policies in pursuit of a middle or third way that discarded Socialism and trade union dominance. Already, under the leadership of Neil Kinnock, the Labour Party policy review of 1989, *Meet the Challenge, Make the Change*, had dropped many of the policies Labour had endorsed in the 1980s, including price and import controls, high income tax, unilateral nuclear disarmament, wealth tax and the restoration of union legal immunities. The review borrowed from Thatcherism in its favourable references to the free market, and it discarded much of the rhetoric and substance of Socialism. This was a key document in the conversion of Labour to the market economy, which was party policy in the 1992 electoral campaign.

In 1994, Blair, the new leader, spoke to the Party conference about his goals: a society 'rich in economic prosperity, secure in social justice, confident in political change' and the linkage of 'New Labour, New Britain'. As shadow Home Secretary in 1992–4, Blair had promised toughness on crime, a policy not hitherto associated with Labour, and one that helped regain the initiative for the Party. This was an aspect of his stress on responsibilities as an aspect of community life, something that Blair had in common with Major. Both sought to temper individualism and permissiveness.

In practice, however, the interventionist role of government remained pronounced. Blair's options were limited by the nature of his parliamentary party, part of which was unconvinced by his policies, and by his focus on foreign policy, particularly after the terrorist attacks on the USA on 11 September 2001. There was also a serious clash between his talk of self-reliance and the reality of a politics that remained keen to see legislation and government as the solution to problems. Both this clash and the widespread failure to solve these problems, for example in health and education provision, contributed to a sense of malaise that was to be accentuated by popular opposition to the armed interventionism of the government abroad.

There was also a persistent clash between ostentatiously proclaimed attempts at modernisation and the reality of the continued dominance of vested interests. Thus, in 2000, Blair announced the appointment of 'people's peers', so that ordinary people could apply to join the House of Lords. In practice, there was no change to the pattern of appointment, other than a marked rise in the proportion of women and members of ethnic minorities.

More generally, uncertain, in the sense of varying, public policy played a role in the marked relative decline of the British economy from the 1940s. This decline was particularly pronounced in manufacturing, although in some sectors, such as pharmaceuticals, British technology remained a market leader. Rapid post-war growth in the economies of Germany, Japan and France helped make Britain appear unsuccessful, and encouraged pressure for Britain to join the European Economic Community (EEC), the basis of the European Union. This was also a reflection of the failure of Britain's global role, as the Empire was transformed into a Commonwealth that could not provide an economic substitute. Instead, Commonwealth states followed their own economic policies which increasingly led Canada to look to the USA, and Australia to Japan. Membership of the EEC, applied for in 1961, was vetoed by France in 1963 in part because Britain was still seen as harbouring global interests. Membership of the EEC was only finally permitted when the government of Edward Heath (1970–4) was willing to abandon most of the Commonwealth special interests, as part of a process in which the agricultural protectionism of the EEC was accepted despite the significant damage it did to British interests. Britain became a member in 1973.

Economic problems contributed to a strong sense of national malaise in the 1960s, 1970s and part of the 1980s. The major devaluation of the pound in 1967, a step long resisted by the Wilson government, contributed to a serious loss of prestige and reflected the extent to which sterling was no longer an attractive reserve currency. More generally, there were also problems due to very high inflation and to a perception of the country as ungovernable, notably in the early 1970s, as strikes by the coal miners led to the failure of government policies on wages. Thereafter, the implications of economic decline were in part kept from the public as a result of the extraction of large quantities of oil from under the North Sea.

However, the defeat of a major miners' strike in 1984–5 was also important as it contributed greatly to a decline in trade union militancy. Thatcher's determined stance against this militancy was important in permitting a recovery of grip after the chaos of much of the 1970s. The miners had been victorious in a strike in 1972, and had helped to cause the fall of the Conservative government of Edward Heath in 1974, making it appear ineffective in the face of union militancy. In contrast, their failure in 1984–5 signalled a marked decline in trade union militancy and in related hopes on the far-left for a collapse of the Thatcher government.

The crisis of mining helped cause unemployment to rise in particular areas, part of the local pattern of economic and social fortunes that is all too easy to forget if the emphasis is on aggregate national trends. These were sombre enough. Unemployment rose from about 1.3 million in 1979 to about 3.5 million in 1983. It was not only that unemployment was highest in traditional mining and heavy industrial areas, such as those that focused on steel and shipbuilding; but also that the highest expenditure per head on income support, and the greatest percentage of households with a low weekly income, was highest in these areas. Alongside the decline of heavy industry, such as steel and shipbuilding, more recent spheres of growth, such as the chemical and car industries, decayed. Transfer payments to the regions with a weaker economy became a key element in public finances. Scotland was a particular beneficiary of transfer payments thanks to the Barnett formula devised in 1978. It was also over-represented, like Wales, in Parliament. Labour benefited greatly from the failure to redistribute parliamentary seats to match the distribution of the population.

Manufacturing decline was matched by shifts in economic activity and the rise in the service sector, and a major change therefore occurred in the experience of work. Management, research and development jobs were increasingly separate from production tasks. The former were concentrated not in traditional manufacturing regions, but in South-East England, in areas such as the M4 corridor west of London, near Cambridge, and, to a lesser extent, in New Towns in southern England, such as Harlow, Milton Keynes and Stevenage. Milton Keynes had the fastest-growing economy outside London between 1997 and 2011. Of the New Towns, it was the one that appealed most to middle-class escapees from London, whereas the first wave of New Towns, such as Stevenage (in 1946, the first planned) and Harlow, were only for council-rented housing.

The 'Establishment' in general became more focused on London and the South-East, with the world of money and services becoming more important than traditional industrial interests, although the City was hit hard by the financial crisis of 2008. The South-East also paid a disproportionately high percentage of taxation, and thus benefited from Thatcher's major cuts in income tax and emphasis on an incentive economy.

No other part of the country saw office development to compare with that in London Docklands in the 1980s. Indeed, One Canada Square, a pyramid-topped 235-metre-high skyscraper in Canary Wharf, built in 1988–91 and then Britain's tallest skyscraper, symbolised the development of the Docklands in East London as a modern business hub focused on financial services. The number of jobs based in the Canary Wharf development quadrupled from 27,400 to 100,500 between 2001 and 2012. As a very different trend, crime also became more linked to financial services.

Development in the South-East was not matched in the North. In 2013, the average yearly earnings of a working man were about £24,000 in the North and about £28,000 in London. In 2013, Lord Howell, a former government energy adviser, caused offence when he suggested that the North-East of England might benefit from shale-gas extraction because it included 'large and uninhabited and desolate areas' where the disruption would not affect people. The following year, the Local Government Association reported that underemployment and underachievement among 16- to 24-year-olds was particularly acute in northern cities, notably Sheffield, Leeds, Newcastle and Manchester. Local authorities that were the worst performing by GCSE exam results in both 2005 and 2012 included authorities in South Yorkshire, Teesside, Liverpool and Manchester, although, in 2012, there were also a range of rural local authorities in this category, including Norfolk, Suffolk, Somerset, Dorset, Herefordshire and Cornwall.

Alongside the City's significance as the prime source of investment capital, the role of the state, in control and regulation, ensured that, whether Labour or the Conservatives were in power, the role of London increased. This owed much to the role of Westminster and Whitehall in determining a unitary British policy agenda, notably after the nationalisation of the Bank of England in 1946 and the creation of the National Health Service in 1948.

Yet, as a reminder of the variety concealed within aggregate regional indices, a variety that was central to the very diverse experience of change, there was, and is, also much poverty in the South-East, not only in London but also along the Thames estuary and in the Medway towns. There were also important local and regional contrasts in Wales and Scotland. Local contrasts were always part of British history, but they became, or appeared, more intense in the 1980s and 1990s, not only due to economic developments but also because of shifts in housing. Council house sales under the 'Right to Buy' legislation of the 1980 Housing Act were widespread but skewed. The better housing in the wealthier areas sold, while the public sector increasingly became 'sink housing', rented by those who suffered relative deprivation. In desperation, local authorities increasingly, from the mid-1990s, demolished such housing, for example in west Newcastle. Local and regional contrasts were also seen in indicators such as the percentage employed by the state, which tends to be greater in the North than the South, as well as in health indicators, such as heart attack rates, which were particularly bad in working-class parts of Scotland.

The rise in the service sector was linked to a growth in consumerism that reflected the rise in prosperity but also owed something to a major extension of personal borrowing that, in turn, was in part a product of technological development, not least in the shape of credit cards and, later, internet purchases. Thanks to the state provision of free or subsidised healthcare, education, council housing, pensions and unemployment pay, rising real incomes fed through into consumption. The percentage of households owning a washing machine rose from 25 in 1958 to 50 in 1964 (88 per cent in 1991), with the dates for cars being 1956 and 1965, and for fridges 1962 and 1968. Purchase tax on consumer durables had been cut from two-thirds to half in 1953, as the Conservatives replaced Labour austerity with affluence and consumer demand. Until the change of policy under Blair, Labour proved cautious about economic individualism and personal affluence, preferring to focus on state-management and public investment.

A consumer and multicultural society

The 1970s saw economic growth hit by serious problems including oil price hikes and trade union militancy; but, in the 1980s and 1990s, a combination of rising real earnings, lower inflation and taxation, and easier credit encouraged spending. Thatcher believed strongly in the need to cut, and value of cutting, personal taxation, and the standard rate of income tax fell from 33 per cent in 1979 to 25 per cent in 1988. Like sport, spending became a major expression of identity and indeed a significant activity in leisure time. The move to 24-hour shopping and the abolition of restrictions on Sunday trading were symptomatic of this shift. The rise of out-of-town retail centres joined consumerism and the car. In 1999, two shopping centres that claimed to be the biggest in Europe were opened: Paisley's 900,000 square-foot Braehead development, and the Bluewater centre in London's Kent suburbs. Towns saw their high streets decline, or at least change, and local traffic patterns changed accordingly, for example in and near Crediton in the early 2010s. By 1999, 88 per cent of all the food purchased in Britain was bought from big shopping chains. In 2003, Tesco, with its 200,000 staff, was the largest private-sector employer in Britain.

Convenience became a key term of the period in both word and thought; and it was adopted as a description, as in convenience foods. This concept was linked to particular forms of packaging, such as wrapping in plastic. It was also linked to a marked decline in the mending of clothes and shoes. This led not only to the closure of cobblers and other outlets but also to a decline in domestic skills such as darning. This decline was part of a major shift in female activity. Cooking, preserving food, knitting and needlework were seen as less important than hitherto as accomplishments, and this was linked to the decline of traditional voluntarist activities.

Shopping patterns reflected social trends in other respects with, for example, a major change in the diet, as red meat declined in relative importance, while lighter meats, fish and vegetarianism all enjoyed greater popularity. So also did products and dishes from around the world, reflecting the extent to which the British had become less parochial and readier to adopt an open attitude. Alongside national trends, however, there were ineluctable facts of social and geographical variation, more specifically issues of class that both the Conservatives and 'New Labour' tended to underplay. Thus, consumption of fresh fruit and vegetables, and fresh (as opposed to fried) fish, is higher among affluent groups, while the poor tend to have less variety and fewer fresh ingredients in their diet. This was an important aspect of a more general crisis of obesity. Takeaway food sales from independent shops fell in the 2000s and 2010s, in part because such shops tended to be in poorer areas. In contrast, sales of supermarket ready meals rose.

There were also pronounced cultural and political variations between social groups, although no full linkage. A YouGov poll in 2014 revealed that on television Conservative voters preferred costume dramas and unchallenging series, notably *Downton Abbey*, *To the Manor Born*, and *Foyle's War*, while Labour voters preferred settings that were more urban and less exalted, notably *Phoenix Nights*, *Coronation Street*, *The Office* and *The Royle Family*.

Aside from food, increased foreign travel and intermarriage were other aspects of a relatively un-xenophobic and continually changing society. Travel was a major focus of consumerism, and one that was actively catered to by newspaper supplements and television programmes. Thanks to high levels of disposable income, and the absence of any restrictions on taking money abroad, the numbers taking holidays abroad rose, from 4.2 million in 1971 to 32.3 million in 1998. Although much of the population never travelled abroad, while large numbers still travelled to traditional destinations, such as Blackpool, domestic tourism became relatively less important. This led to a changing sense of place for many, one that bridged Britain and abroad. Glaswegians who went to Majorca, rather than Largs, and Londoners who travelled to Cyprus, not Cornwall or Scotland, now had a different experience of their own countries.

Foreign lifestyles and travel were also related to the marked growth in cut-price air travel in the 2000s, although the government pushed the cost up by taxing air tickets. Technology and organisational improvements joined to consumerism to produce lower costs as well as profit. Prices were cut in part by the more efficient use of planes and crew, and, in part by removing the need for travel agents by encouraging the direct purchase of tickets, by credit card, over the phone or via the internet. This was an aspect of the more general move away from a face-to-face society. Cut-price air travel, moreover, led to a new geography of communications, as airports that were its centres, such as Luton and Stansted, became more important. This was an instance of the manner in which the experience of Britain as a set of places and routes has changed radically over the last three centuries, and is continuing to alter rapidly.

Owing in part to travel, most of British society was far less prejudiced and racist than critics frequently suggested, and notably so in terms of international comparisons. Indeed, a tolerant multi-culturalism characterises much of British life, particularly in England, and is one definition of its society. From the 1980s, a new style of speech called Multicultural London English, a hybrid of West India, South Asian and native English styles, became increasingly common in London, with variants in other cities with numerous immigrants.

The open-ended nature of this society, the sense that change and continuity were a joint dynamic, was one under challenge from differing definitions of this dynamic, but there was, and is, an overall willingness to accept this formulation of nation and country. Indeed national values, or rather classic stereotypes of these values, changed, with a decline in the practice of restraint ('stiff upper lip') readily apparent in the public response to the tragic death in 1997 of Diana, Princess of Wales. The Protestantism and low-key racism, both significant in established social practice, also became less important. Instead, there was an emphasis on tolerance and multi-culturalism as both goals for, and means of, nationhood. If 59 per cent of Britons called themselves Christian on census forms, there was scant hostility towards religious minorities.

At the same time, there is room for considerable concern about elements of the future, and this concern is relevant to the historian, both because it is part of the recent past and as it forms a comment on it. The range of concern reflects the diversity of public views, but several major themes can be discerned. They include the human impact on the environment, an issue that became fashionable in the 1960s and newly-significant in the 2000s as evidence mounted of global warming. That warming may have played a role in the serious storms and heavy rainfall of the winter of 2013–14, storms that revealed the vulnerability of transport and power systems and rainfall that caused widespread flooding.

Concern over the environment was linked to particular anxieties over air quality and, as in 2006, to the availability of sufficient water. In 2003, activists stopped the growing of genetically modified crops. Moreover, in 2013 there were protests against shale gas exploration; and the possibility that this issue would affect the next general election was raised in 2014.

Concern over the human impact on the environment also reflected worry about rising population numbers, particularly in southern England. Thus, worry about the natural environment was related to that over the human/built environment, with quality of life under pressure from a sense of crowding. Longstanding attempts to make urban life at a high rate of population density normative encountered continued resistance, not only from the widespread desire for suburban life at a lower density but also from the reality of urban problems including concern about crime and, in many areas, worry about educational provision.

In some places, such concerns were related to anxieties about the impact of large-scale immigration. This was one of the most significant changes in modern Britain. Whereas immigration has been central to the American experience and world-view from the outset, the political, social and cultural impact of immigration into modern Britain did not become prominent until the 1950s. As a consequence, the process by which the empire formally 'came home' proved troubling to many.

Anxieties about large-scale immigration gathered renewed pace in the early twenty-first century. In particular, Poland joining the EU in 2004 was followed by large-scale immigration from there. The impact of a changing composition of the population was accentuated because, from the early 1990s, births had come so close to deaths and emigration that the total number of the native population has been constant, at about 52 million. As a result, most of the population growth was due to immigration, the number of non-natives living in Britain rising from 4.8 million in 1995 to 13.4 million in 2011. Of these, the 729,000 Indian-born inhabitants were the largest group, followed by the 646,000 Poles. In the last three months of 2013, the number of those born in Bulgaria and Romania who were working in Britain rose by over 40 per cent to 144,000. The resulting pressure on the labour market, particularly for low-skilled jobs, exacerbated the impact of new technology. In April 2014, the unemployment rate was 6.5 per cent. However, immigrants also provided labour skills and tax revenues and countered the structure of an ageing native population. Moreover, the euro area unemployment rate in May 2014 was 11.6 per cent and that of the USA in June was 6.1 per cent.

The consequences of immigration provided a major theme for British culture, whether the genealogical programmes that were increasingly popular on television, or in novels or plays. Thus, *England People Very Nice*, a play by Richard Bean staged at the National Theatre in 2009, dealt with the waves of immigration to Bethnal Green, a cockpit of London's East End: Huguenots, Irish, Jews, Bangladeshis and Somalis. At one level, the play is about assimilation, with immigrants becoming Cockneys, so that the barmaid ends up as a woman of Irish-French extraction married to a Jew and with grandchildren who are half-Bangladeshi. At the same time, there are darker currents which are far from hidden. First, there is the backdrop of a xenophobic mob angry at the Huguenots for taking jobs, the Irish for being Catholics, and the Jews for producing Jack the Ripper (for which there is only problematic evidence), and also accusing the Bangladeshis of being 'curried monkeys'. The far-right British National Party is an element in the story. Even darker are the young Bangladeshis in the last act who lack their elders' willingness to accept British values. The youngsters, in contrast, hate the other British as infidels, admire Osama bin Laden, and seek a British caliphate, with the intolerance and bloodshed that entails. Bean's play captured central questions about Britain's ability to go on coping with its diversity.

The character of the country changed greatly as a consequence of rising immigration. Polls in the early 2010s indicated that only a small percentage among ethnic minorities were willing to vote Conservative. In addition, most saw themselves as British, rather than the English identity that the white indigenous population was readier to express. Moreover, it was suggested that levels of immigration and differential birth rates were such that by 2050 nearly a third of the population would be from ethnic minorities.

Alongside these issues, there are concerns about the sustainability of current assumptions, whether in the shape of pension provisions that are under mounting pressure from greater longevity and the resulting ageing population, the assumption that there will be sufficient housing, or expectations about the international influence that Britain can, or should, have. The extent of borrowing raised major questions about sustainability. The current account deficit in 2014 stood at £111.7 billion, which was the equivalent of 4.0 per cent of GDP, while the budget deficit was 4.6 per cent of GDP.

There was a broader question about the future of the economy. Output fell markedly in 2008–9, by about 7 per cent, and by 2013, despite a recovery in exports, had still not returned to 2007 figures. In the meanwhile, output per worker fell by nearly 4 per cent, while, before rising in 2014, real wages fell by 7.8 per cent. This created a (justified) sense of being poorer, which was matched by the crisis in social capital caused by the need to cut government expenditure in order to deal with the budget deficit. Borrowing led to a highly risky position for Britain's credit, and, thus, its viability. By September 2009, the national debt stood at £804.4 billion, equivalent to over £25,000 per every family in Britain.

This situation created a potent tranche of discontent, one mined for political advantage by populists across the political spectrum. High-tax strategies and those focused on controlling prices, for example for energy, tended to be singularly careless of the pressures of the global economy and of Britain's need for investment.

Concerns about the future were accentuated in the 2010s by the clear inability of the EU to meet the expectations of many about the direction of European policy, and by anxieties about the ability of society to accommodate the demands of its diverse constituents. None of these issues can be readily accommodated to a comfortable or conventional account of national history. That, indeed, is a major part of this recent history.

CHAPTER SIX

Conclusions

Uncertainty is the dominant theme in the 2010s, uncertainty with reference to Britain's relations within both the European Union and British Isles, the challenge of terrorism, and the very nature of a society greatly affected by immigration at a hitherto unprecedented rate. There is also growing concern about the state and direction of the environment. More generally, goals and achievements seemed out of line, as the usual contrast between the aspirations and the reality of government appeared particularly glaring in response to the overspun nature of the former, and a public much of which was well-informed about, and sensitive to, failings. A series of corruption scandals involving parliamentarians, notably the revelation in 2009 of large-scale fiddling of expenses, corroded confidence in Parliament.

At the same time as there was concern over whether the government, indeed of whatever party, knew how best to define and sustain a viable interpretation of the national interest and national interests, so the sense of national identity was very much under challenge. This created uncertainty, and also led to a tension over how best to present national history. The last was a matter not only of specifics, such as the treatment of the slave trade and of World War One, but also the questions of the general interpretation and presentation of national history, as well as the extent to which a single nation, country, indeed state, could, and should, be discerned in British history.

This point is of major concern because arguments for Irish, Scottish and Welsh nationalism are heavily historicist and, in part, rest on the notion that Britishness is an extension of Englishness, or is employed by the English to that end. This, however, is an argument that makes little sense of the processes by which Britishness has been defined and redefined. Moreover, Britishness is an aspect of a multiple sense of identities, and not one that excludes all others. Both recent and more distant history were debated and revised while these issues were probed.

Such contention is far from new, nor confined to this issue. For example, within the memory of many readers, Margaret Thatcher, Prime Minister from 1979 to 1990, and her supporters, rejected the analysis of economic planning and management, and thus of recent history, offered by the influential economist John Maynard Keynes, views that had been very important in the three previous decades. Instead, in the 1980s, Keynesian economics, particularly deficit financing (government borrowing), was condemned for a willingness to accept dangerous levels of inflation, which was seen as socially disruptive. Furthermore, Thatcher argued that both Conservative and Labour governments had failed to restrain trade union power. In turn, explicitly Keynesian remedies were endorsed in the late 2000s, notably by the Brown government, in response to the economic and fiscal crisis of the period.

In her reputation, Thatcher herself reflected the lack of any fixity in historical memory. Much criticised while Prime Minister, and subsequently, she became, by the time of her death in 2013, a figure treated as an example across much of the political spectrum. Blair commented on ITN on 8 April 2013: 'I think the trade union framework, the privatisation of certain industries, and some of the things that she did in relation to tax and spending, this is part of the common political consensus now'. At the same time, there was also much criticism of her administration in 2013.

The abiding tendency of both government and much public history, for example that offered on the television, was, and is, a maladroit and misleading reluctance to accept the variety of possible interpretations when offering an overall account. Instead, there is a preference for clear simplicity. This preference is mistaken. There is room for debate, not only over very different readings of the recent past but also as a result of tensions over the longer-term interpretation of British history.

Four particular themes command attention, each linking the long term to more recent controversies. First, there is the question of how far and with what consequences Britain is a European country, and how far it is appropriate to see a different pattern of development and, indeed, a distinctive framework for analysis. Second, there is the relationship between Britain, England, Scotland and Wales. Third, there is tension over the nature of liberty that is seen as particularly British, and, in particular, the relationship between liberties and collectivism. The latter is a challenge, if not, sometimes, threat, to both liberties and the theory and practice of freedom. Fourth, there is the question of the role of religion in national identity, and this, in part, is related to discussion of issues of ethnicity and nationality.

In no case is it possible to point to agreement on these points. That, itself, is part of the history of the country, and not least because a relative freedom of debate has been a characteristic of British politics since the suppression of Jacobitism in the mid-eighteenth century. Definitions of freedom clearly vary, and there are opinions that would now be seen as reasonable that earlier could not be readily expressed publicly, as stage censorship amply showed. Indeed, the parameters of political and social discussion varied greatly. Nevertheless, Britain has a long tradition of freedom of expression. Pre-publication censorship in England ended with the lapsing of the Licensing Act in 1695, and, albeit with serious limitations during the revolutionary crisis of the 1790s, it was possible to express very critical views, with, for example, a late nineteenth-century upsurge in republican sentiment.

At the same time, the tendency for the expression of diverse views was accentuated in the twentieth century by the combination of the decline of deference and hierarchy in society, the expansion of further and higher education, and rising prosperity which, for example, ensured that those who wished it had ready access to news products. By 1994, 99 per cent of British households had televisions, with 96 per cent having colour televisions. In 2011, 92 per cent of the UK population owned a mobile phone, while 80 per cent of UK homes had internet access and 60 per cent could plug into superfast broadband.

In recent decades, the expression of diverse views has been accentuated because of the decline of respect, not least for ideas and institutions that had acted for many as orthodoxies, for example churches, the monarchy, the rule of law, trade unions and political parties. All of this has made debate over values less predictable.

Past practices certainly appeared disposable as part of the contract between people and government that was increasingly seen as a key aspect of British society. Transparency, advanced against official secrets in a series of political and legal battles from the 1970s, was an aspect of the explicit contracts encouraged by the Major government (1990–7) and then advocated under its successors in order to spur reform in the public sector. Performance targets were seen as a way to guide institutional improvement and personal choice. Satisfaction surveys combined with market research and the use of focus groups to promote a sense of responsive and democratised businesses and public services. Market research was applied to government and politics. By 2012, information was freely available on school results, university student satisfaction, crime patterns, transport delays and medical performance. The leaflet published in 2010 by the Office for National Statistics presented the 2011 census for England and Wales as a form of empowerment:

> It's time to complete your census questionnaire. The census collects information about the population every ten years. You need to take part so that services in your area – like schools, hospitals, housing, roads and emergency services – can be planned and funded for the future. Help tomorrow take shape.

There was also the blunter reminder of authority – 'Your census response is required by law' – as well as two pages providing details on how to obtain copies of the questions in a variety of languages, from Akan to Yoruba. No one was to be missed out, not least because claims of under-registration played a major role in demands by inner-city boroughs that they receive larger governmental grants.

While available information on the present increased, the public sense of continuity with the past was lessened. Many of the policies of the Blair government (1997–2007) reflected a sense that the past could, indeed should, be readily discarded, and that the future could be readily shaped without reference to historical continuity, that indeed the latter was anachronistic and the product of past invention: 'New Labour' sought to 'repackage' national identity with soundbites such as 'New Britain' and 'A Young Country'. Symbolically, it was decided at a very senior ministerial level under the Blair government to include no selection on history in the Millennium Dome at Greenwich. Longstanding constitutional, political and governmental practices, were altered, particularly with the composition of the House of Lords and the governance of Scotland and Wales.

As a result of referenda in 1997, Scotland, in 1999, acquired a Parliament, with a substantial legislative programme on domestic affairs and with tax-varying powers, while Wales acquired an Assembly. Considerable differences between Scotland and England swiftly opened up, notably as a result of the different cost structures put in place under the 2001 Graduate Endowment and Student Support, and Regulation of Care, Acts. In turn, coverage of Scottish and Welsh news in the national news broadcast from London diminished. Scotland was termed a 'region', to the irritation of the Scots. This continued a tendency seen from the Scottish perspective in which Scotland had been regionalised from the 1940s as Great Britain ceased to be imperial and multinational and, instead, became an English-dominated Little Britain. There was certainly less English interest in Scottish culture than had been the case in the Victorian period. Whereas Sir Walter Scott (1771–1832) and Robert Burns (1759–96) had been very significant writers for English school curricula into the 1930s, by the 1960s both had been discarded. In turn, much of Scottish culture became more inward-looking.

The 'New Labour project' was superficial from the outset and, as it greyed, its strictures and proposals appeared increasingly redundant. This was particularly so with the issue of Englishness, with which the government was very uncomfortable, attempting, instead, to offer a duality of regionalism and Britishness. Labour's attempt to introduce regional assemblies in England was, however, unsuccessful, unlike the creation of the Greater London Assembly, a revival of the GLC (Greater London Council) abolished under Thatcher. The role of sport, particularly football, in expressing and strengthening Englishness was therefore of wider political significance insofar as it expressed concern about a lack of identity within a Britain that was apparently increasingly driven, under Labour, by an agenda moulded by Scottish and Welsh perceptions and interests.

Regionalism had little purchase in the British imagination, unlike the localism seen in England with its strong continuing commitment to counties, which are a key survival from the

Anglo-Saxon period. However, this localism has been drained of impact by the extent to which central government has taken control of public life, and indeed influence over private life. This is a major contrast with the USA where the role of the states offers a continuance of older English roots that, in contrast, have become attenuated in Britain.

Localism was also weakened by social, economic and cultural developments. Lord Somerhayes, a Northumbrian landowner presented as an anachronistic figure in Alan Hunter's novel *Landed Gently* (1957), has a strong sense of the historicity of place and people:

> 'That way came the Northmen!' exclaimed Somerhayes in a strange ringing tone. 'On a day like this, on a wind like this, in ships without decks, they sailed that sea, Mr Gently. A thousand years ago one saw their dragon sails, and a few last descendants of those ships still sail the Northshire rivers. Go into any fishing village along this coast, and look, and you will see the Northmen ... We Feverells come of Norman stock, but whence came the Normans to set their standard in France?'.

Such attitudes appeared in 1957, and still appear, outdated, and notably in England; although there was a degree of ethno-genesis in the argument for Scottish nationalism.

The failure of the 'New Labour project' directed attention to the need both to recover an understanding of national history and to avoid facile criticisms of this history. Both the Labour government of Gordon Brown (2007–10), and its Conservative-dominated coalition successor under David Cameron (2010–15), sought to emphasise Britishness and to encourage the teaching of national history. The process proved controversial, but many of the criticisms of Britain's history are ahistorical in tone and content, notably those that often deliberately challenge patriotism.

In practice, the history of Britain and the British has always been interesting, has over the last millennium been more generally important, was crucial over the last quarter-millennium, and has often been both glorious and praiseworthy. This is the case not only with reference to past values but also, particularly, in the comparative context. It is difficult to consider episodes such as the cruelties and destruction of the French, Russian and Chinese revolutions, the slaughter of the American Civil War, and the genocidal character of German imperialism, without feeling that the crimes attributed to British power, while serious, are relatively modest.

Furthermore, the quest for freedom, the defence of liberty, and the respect for both law and individual rights, that provide both narrative and analysis, not for the entire thrust of British history in some Whiggish fashion, but rather for important episodes in it, offer a noteworthy example both to the present and, more generally, across the world. It is the peculiar greatness of British history that those who fought gloriously for national independence, most epically in 1805 and 1940, but also in a host of lesser-known episodes, were also asserting values that were more noble and important than those of the nation's enemies.

At the same time, the confidence expressed in such views appeared increasingly precarious by the 2010s. There was a degree of recovery from the economic and financial crisis of the late 2000s, but much of the population was affected by anxieties about their living conditions, notably the availability of housing and employment. There was a widespread sense that children no longer had as good a prospect as their parents and, notably due to the difficulty of obtaining attractive, or even any, housing, this was certainly the case for a significant percentage. In 2013, three million people aged between 20 and 34 were still living at home with their parents, while there were 289,000 families housing another family under their roof, often young couples living with a parent.

The possibility of discontent had been indicated by riots in London in 2011, riots in which anger with the police and looting for consumer goods both played a role. At the same time, by 2014 it was the limited rate of such discontent and the falling crime rate that was more notable. The riots also indicated the extent to which technology affected options. The rioters co-ordinated disorder by mobile phone and smartphone use, and encrypted their communications, which handicapped the police response.

Tension between the generations was less pronounced for many than anxieties about identity focusing on concerns about immigration and also about relations with the rest of the EU. Such anxieties were particularly expressed by the elderly. This group, which was demographically more pronounced, became politically more prominent in the 2010s. The absence of confidence at times appeared paranoid, at times almost an aspect of nervous exhaustion, but it also reflected a sense that the established national narrative of greatness and achievement, however flawed and partial, could not capture the experience and commitment of many who were scarcely political radicals. This was a part of the lack of certainty over national history that was readily apparent in the 2010s.

NOTE

1400–1750

1 Lyttelton, *Letters* (4th edn, London, 1735), pp. 221–2.

SELECTED FURTHER READING

The following is necessarily a selective list, concentrating on recent books. Other books and articles can be traced through the bibliographies to these books.

1 General

T. Bartlett, *Ireland: A History* (2010).

T. M. Charles-Edwards, *Wales and the Britons, 350–1064* (2013).

A. Cronin and L. O'Callaghan, *A History of Ireland* (2nd edn, 2014).

M. Lynch (ed.), *The Oxford Companion to Scottish History* (2011).

F. Pryor, *The Birth of Modern Britain: A Journey into Britain's Archaeological Past, 1550 to the Present* (2011).

I. G. Simmons, *An Environmental History of Great Britain* (2001).

K. Tiller and G. Darkes (eds), *An Historical Atlas of Oxfordshire* (2010).

2 To 1400

J. L. Bolton, *Money in the Medieval English Economy, 973–1489* (2012).

A. D. Carr, *Medieval Wales* (1995).

K. J. Edwards and I. B. M. Ralston (eds), *Scotland: Environment and Archaeology, 8000 BC–AD 1000* (1997).

B. Goldring, *Conquest and Colonisation: The Normans in Britain, 1066–1100* (2nd edn, 2012).

H. Hamerow *et al.* (eds), *Oxford Handbook of Anglo-Saxon Archaeology* (2011).

J. Hudson, *The Oxford History of the Laws of England, II. 871–1216* (2012).

W. M. Ormrod, *Political Life in Medieval England, 1300–1450* (1995).
M. L. Prestwich, *English Politics in the Thirteenth Century* (1990).
N. Vincent, *The Birth of the Nation: 1066–1485* (2012).

3 1400–1750

G. Burgess, *British Political Thought, 1500–1660* (2009).
S. J. Connolly, *Divided Kingdom: Ireland, 1630–1800* (2010).
I. Gentles, *Oliver Cromwell* (2011).
W. Gibson, *The Making of the Nation, 1660–1851* (2012).
S. Gunn, *Early Tudor Government, 1485–1558* (1995).
A. Hughes, *The Causes of the English Civil War* (2nd edn, 1998).
J. G. Jones, *Early Modern Wales, c. 1525–1640* (1994).
D. MacCulloch, *The Later Reformation in England, 1547–1603* (1990).
A. Walsham, *The Reformation of the Landscape: Religion, Identity and Memory in Early Modern Britain and Ireland* (2011).

4 1750–1900

E. Biagini, *Gladstone* (1994).
J. Black, *Eighteenth-Century Britain* (2nd edn, 2008).
P. Buckner (ed.), *Canada and the British Empire* (2010).
T. A. Jenkins, *Sir Robert Peel* (1999).
J. MacCaffrey, *Scotland in the Nineteenth Century* (1998).
I. Machin, *The Rise of Democracy in Britain, 1830–1918* (2001).
J. Mokyr, *The Enlightened Economy: An Economic History of Britain, 1700–1850* (2009).
A. Murdoch, *British History, 1600–1832: National Identity and Local Culture* (1998).
M. Pittock, *Jacobitism* (1998).

5 1900–present

J. Black, *Britain Since the Seventies* (2004).
D. G. Boyce, *The Irish Question and British Politics, 1868–1996* (2nd edn, 1996).
C. Brown, *Religion and Society in Twentieth-Century Britain* (2006).
S. Bruley, *Women in Britain since 1900* (1999).

W. H. Fraser, *A History of British Trade Unionism, 1700–1998* (1999).

D. Gladstone, *The Twentieth-Century Welfare State* (1999).

H. Goulbourne, *Race Relations in Britain since 1945* (1998).

B. Harrison, *Seeking a Role: The United Kingdom, 1951–1970* (2011).

B. Harrison, *Finding a Role? The United Kingdom, 1970–1990* (2011).

A. Jackson, *The Two Unions: Ireland, Scotland, and the Survival of the United Kingdom, 1707–2007* (2011).

B. Jackson and R. Saunders (eds), *Making Thatcher's Britain* (2012).

R. McKibbin, *Parties and People: England, 1914–1951* (2011).

A. Thorpe, *A History of the British Labour Party* (2nd edn, 2001).

INDEX